A DAISY IN THE WHEAT FIELD

By Koralee Jaspers

In Memory of my Grandparents:

Palmer Olai Helgren & Alice Beatrice Hoversten

Loved by all for their generosity and loving kindness!

Copyright © 2020 by Koralee Jaspers

All rights reserved.

No part of this book may be reproduced in any form or by any electronic or mechanical means, including information storage and retrieval systems, without written permission from the author, except for the use of brief quotations in a book review.

ISBN: 978-1-716-25166-5

The Story of our Heritage

Our ancestors were part of a massive movement of people to a New World. 38 million left their native land to immigrate to America in the early 1800's and 1900's. We marvel at these hard-working men, women, and children willing to endure suffering and hardship for the hope of a better life. With faith they zealously and courageously plunged into the unknown, struggling to survive. They let nothing hinder them. Neither prejudice, nor the barrier of language could stop them. Our ancestors accepted and met the challenges of life head on, praying for wisdom and the strength to succeed. They enjoyed the simple pleasures of life. Humor, hospitality, true friends and the wonders of creation added much to their happiness. The trials and sorrows of their neighbors were their own. Hardship and tears often became the language of their heart, yet they endured. Hundreds of years now separate us from them, yet we still enjoy a special bond. How blessed we are for their outstanding faith, courage and loving sacrifices! Remarkable too, is the tribute paid by the family members left behind in their homeland!

In the city park of Stavanger, Norway stands a statue with the inscription, "Dedicated to the men and women of Norwegian blood who contributed to the building of America."

characters (highlighted in bold)

Helgren Family
Johannes Anton Joseph Hellgren-changed name to **John Helgren** when he came to America at the age of 19. Born in Ystad, Sweden on Nov. 25, 1867. Died on Feb. 3, 1950 at the age of 83. His favorite saying: "A man is as good as his word."
(John's parents: Peter Hellgren-born April 6, 1833, Bertha born Oct. 4, 1830)
(John's siblings: Olaf born 1859, Anna 1862, Ida 1872, Nils 1883)
Martha Carrie Hanson was born near Decorah, Iowa, on March 30, 1868 and died Feb. 3, 1943. (parents: Ole Hanson & Carrie Donhowe) Carrie died in 1871 when Martha was 2 years old. Martha had a sister named **Lizzie**. Martha's 3 brothers: Hans died at age 7, Ole age 5, Carl age 1.
John & Martha were married March 10, 1892 at the North Prairie Church near Lake Mills, Iowa. They farmed 2 miles west of Thompson, IA. They had 7 children: **Palmer Olai** born Sept. 14, 1893, died May 5, 1930 at age 36.
Clarence Bernhard, **Mabel** Josephine, **Hazel** Jeanette, **Myrtle** Claretta, **Leonard** Joseph and Helen Margaret.

Hoversten Family
Edward Hoversten was born on Rennesoy Island near Stavanger, Norway in 1859. He died Nov. 28, 1931 at the age of 72.
Tobia Anderson was born in Ramsfjeld, Norway on June 30, 1859 and died Oct. 22, 1942 at the age of 83. She married Edward on Aug. 15, 1882 in Norway. They came to America on July 16, 1892 at the age of 33. Their farm was southeast of Thompson. They had 6 children:
Anna was born Oct. 22, 1882 in Norway. She died March 22, 1935 at age 52. She married **Michael Risa** in 1911. They farmed near Hanley Falls, MN. They had 8 children: **Amy** born Jan. 22, 1912, **Olaf** 1914, **Thelma**, April 21, 1915, **Elmer** Sept. 10, 1916, **Mildred**, 1921, **Helen**, Feb. 22, 1923, **Arlen** Nov.5, 1924, **Ethel**, April 3, 1926.
Inger was born Aug. 17, 1885 in Norway. She died Nov. 18, 1943, at age 58. She married **Hawkin Berven** in 1912. They farmed near Thompson. They had 3 children: **Allen** born Feb 17, 1920, **Eunice**, Harold born Aug. 23, 1932.
Jennie was born March 6, 1893 and died Dec. 19, 1952 at age 59. She married **Martin Thompson**. They farmed near Williams, Iowa.
Jacob was born Nov. 1, 1896 and died Jan. 7, 1992 at age 95. He married **Edna** Bryan in 1917. They had 4 children: **Ardis** born Dec. 29, 1919, **Norrene** 1922, **Raymond** Feb.16, 1924, Margery March 9, 1928.

Elmer was born Oct 19, 1898 and died Nov. 1984 at age 86. He married Josephine (**Josie**) Sunde in 1922. They had 4 children: **Robert** born June 9, 1923, died 1944. **Vivian** born Oct. 21, 1924, **Leslie** born March 13, 1926, Bonnie born May 8, 1935. **Alice** born Dec. 26, 1903 and died April 29, 1960 at the age of 56. Married Palmer Helgren, October 30, 1922. They farmed near Thompson, Iowa. They had 3 children: Ernest (**Ernie**) born May 10, 1923, Marvin (**Marv**) born May 9, 1925 and **Helen Palmere** born April 29, 1930.

Threshing Crew
Walter Carson: best man at Palmer & Alice's wedding
Eli Olafsen: works at John's Blacksmith Shop & known for his strength
Bjorn Livingston
Hans Peterson: nickname Fox
Olaf Hanson: nickname Plowboy
Jake Anderson: sings & plays fiddle
Oscar Vage: Palmer's hired man

Gunvor Torgeson & son Ole: neighbors to Ed & Tobia Hoversten
Elias & Emma Erickson: owners of the General Store
Gyda Yawnson: reputation for gossip
Bertina Fardel: Gyda's telephone accomplice
Karina Anderson: Thompson's Telephone Operator
Michael Kirke: Sheriff for King township
Doc Allison & daughters: Rachel (midwife) Mary (married to Walter Carson) & Malenda (Mary's twin)
Peter Ellwood: wealthy farmer & owner of horse ranch
Vage family: Oscar, Sadie, (children) Sarah, Ruth, David, (twins Leah & Lydia) Rachel, (twins Joel & Jonathan)
Nabal Zinnser: Palmer's hired man

Chapter 1 The Handsome Stranger

Summer of 1922
Thompson, Iowa

Alice heard the dog barking and peeked out the kitchen window. "Someone's coming in on a black horse," she announced.
Alice's mother, Tobia peeked over her shoulder. "Ja, vho dat be?" She called to her husband, Edward, "Ve git compane!"
Ed got up slowly from the supper table. "Ja, dat vud be Palmer Helgren. He kustom thrasherman. I kantrakt to git veat out."
Alice's parents had lived in America for many years, but still had the Norwegian accent of their homeland. When they tried to speak in English it came out with a sort of brogue. But Papa was determined to speak English. He was always telling Mama, "Ve liv' in Amarika now, ve got to spe'k lik' dey do." He ambled outside as Palmer dismounted from his black gelding.
"Dat shore is goodt lukin' felo, Alice. Vadda ye tink?"
Alice peered out the window at a tall, slender stranger. He took off his straw hat and ran his fingers through his blonde hair. The evening breeze lifted his wavy hair and set it back down in disarray.
"I wonder if his eyes are blue," said Alice with a dreamy expression on her face.
"I tink so, he luk lik' a Swede." Tobia turned back to the stove where Alice had been cooking lefse on the hot griddle. " Gerl, ye burnt da lefse vil ye makin' kow eyes at dat handsom' stranjer."
Alice dragged her eyes away from the window, grabbed the lefse stick and flipped it off the griddle. "Dat von burnt so bad not even da hogs vil eat it," chuckled Tobia. Then they both burst into laughter.
"Mother, you should know by now. I always seem to burn the last piece. It's a tradition around here," giggled Alice.
"Ooo, vel ve hav' plente."
Alice turned back to the window in eager anticipation, but the stranger was gone. Disappointed she turned back to her lefse and then she heard voices on the front porch.
"Alice, spred som' but'er an' shuger on dat lefse. I tink ve hav' evnin' gest. I git da glasiz' an' lemenad'."
Alice quickly fixed the lefse just the way Papa loved it. Her head was spinning! Should she take off her apron? She looked down at her blue work dress, old and

faded. In an instant, she decided her new blue-checkered-gingham apron was a necessary fashion accessory. Alice tried to tuck in the loose ends of her hair, but Mama was calling, "Alice, brin' da lefse!"

Balancing a plate in her hand and some cloth napkins in the other, she charged out the door, bumping into the handsome stranger. She looked up into a charming face with two sparkling, sky-blue eyes and a big, bright smile. Palmer felt his heart leap as he stared into Alice's big, brown eyes so full of life. Her sweet face was like a breath of fresh air on this warm summer evening. Tobia had set the lemonade tray down on a small table and sat down next to Ed.

"Mr. Helgren, tis mi vif' Tobia an' mi doter Alice. Dis Palmer Helgren. He goin' to thrash aur veat."

Palmer graciously took Tobia's hand in his. "It's nice to meet you and your lovely daughter, Mrs. Hoversten."

Tobia tried to say, 'I am very glad to meet you,' but her Norwegian slipped out. "Det var hyggelig a treffe deg."

Ed barked, "spe'k English!"

Tobia tried again, "Hape to meet ye."

"P'eas' sit down an' rest a spel', Mr. Helgren," invited Ed.

Alice standing there staring, thought Mama might be right. She was makin' cow-eyes at this tall, handsome stranger. She had to get these inappropriate, flirtatious instincts under control.

"Alice dun't yust stan' dere. Serv' dis youn' felo som' lefse, lest he starv'," Tobia suggested.

With trembling hands, Alice served the lemonade and lefse.

"Alice is a mite fin' kuk. Dat is if ve kin ke'p her in da kitshun," chuckled Ed taking a bite of lefse.

"She be outsid' sins da day she larn to valk," explained Tobia. "Alvays mes' vith da liv'stak, garden an' flauers."

"I can't say I blame her. I love wide open spaces," said Palmer winking at Alice.

"Ja, Alice vas aur surpris' babe," laughed Ed.

Alice felt impending trouble! She silently pleaded, *'Papa please don't tell this story!'* Her stomach did a flip-flop!

Ed continued, "Ve thot ve vas dun aft'r da boys an' den out pops lit'l Alice!"

Tobia cut him off. "Edward, babes dun't yust pop out! Birthin' is hardt vork!" She looked at Palmer and explained, "I vas ol' vomen when I hav' Alice, 'mos' kil' me."

Alice felt her cheeks turning flaming red. The butterflies in her stomach were doing barrel rolls.

Ed loved to tell stories and he pressed on. "I 'no', but ye se' Alice vas numb'r siks, a f'iste, lit'l skrap'r an' she dun't mes' araund." Ed bellowed with laughter!
Alice felt her butterflies going into a tailspin!!
Ed continued, "I see her lit'l he'd comin'. It luk lik' a krumpl'd valnut shel', but lik' I sez, vhen it pop out it vas da purtest lit'l pink he'd ye ever did se'."
Alice butterflies were screaming, "MAYDAY!!! MAYDAY!!!"
"She vas slipere as fresh churn'd but'er, but I ketch her in mi big hands."
Alice was sure her butterflies would crash and burn any time now!!!
Ed laughed, "Ve had tings al' vrap'd up bi da tim' da mid-vif' git dere!"
Alice glanced at Palmer and he seemed to be enjoying this story way too much. He was grinning ear to ear. Alice struggled to swallow. She needed to change the subject before her butterflies crashed.
"Best surpris' ve ever had, rit Moder?" said Ed tenderly.
"Ja, Edward ye aur alvays rit," chuckled Tobia.
Alice mind worked frantically! She quickly ordered her butterflies into flying formation. *'Alley-oop, up and away!'* With her heart pounding in her throat, she looked into Palmer's sky-blue eyes and asked, "Do you have any children?" Alice knew her face was as red as the setting sun. *Why on earth did I ask such a foolish thing?* She felt her butterflies' tailspin, spiraling straight for earth.
Palmer's face radiated a huge smile. He struggled to suppress his laughter as he said, "No children, Miss Alice, I'm not married."
Ed asked, "How com'? A goodt lukin' felo lik' ye must atrak youn' lad'es lik' flies to a shuger bowl."
Palmer answered, "I don't really get too many opportunities to meet young ladies in the wheat fields."
"Ja, dere's not mane gerls on da thrashing kru e'ther," chuckled Ed. "But mi Alice, she's mi rit-hand man. Ve ben out in dat veat field fer a 'hol' vek. Ve git dose shocks of veat al rede fer thrashin' day."
"What kind of reaper do you have Mr. Hoversten?" asked Palmer.
"It McCormick re'per. It sur' do vork goodt. It sur' do vork bet'r den ol' sc'ith'."
"Yes, it's a wonderful invention." Palmer reached down and picked up his hat lying next to his chair. "I better be on my way." He had noticed his horse was getting impatient, stamping and sidling about. "Pepper is doing his been-here-long-enough dance. Thank you for the pleasant company, lemonade and the lefse was delicious, Alice."
Alice gazed into Palmer's sun-tanned face. His tousled blonde hair had fallen down on his forehead, again. His eyes sparkled and his bright smile showed off his

perfect white teeth. It set her butterflies all in a flutter! Wooziness swept over her again. Alice felt like her tongue had grown long and her naughty butterflies had tied it into a double knot. Not trusting herself, she simply nodded with a big smile. Palmer turned his attention back to Ed. "Mr. Hoversten, if those golden shocks of wheat are ready and waiting, it's time to bring them in. I'll be back early tomorrow with the threshing machine and crew. Good Evening."
Ed called after him, "Takk ye, Mr. Helgren! Ve se' ye in da mornin'."
Alice couldn't help but wish he could stay longer. There was so much she wanted to know about this man. The handsome young stranger mounted his horse, tipped his hat and disappeared into the evening shadows.

Chapter 2   A Flower in the Wheat Field

There he was again. The handsome stranger with the leather band on his straw hat. And peeking out from under the brim were his dreamy eyes, blue as the sky, twinkling like two evening stars. He wore a white cotton shirt with rolled up sleeves that exposed his strong sun-tanned arms. His dark jeans covered his muscular thighs. He was mounted on his valiant, black steed with his shiny leather boots in the stirrups.

"COCK-A-DOODLE-DO!!!" Henry was exercising his lungs with his morning cry.

I hate that rooster, thought Alice. If she had her way, Henry would be next in the stewpot. Alice pried open one eye and saw the first rays of morning light coming through her bedroom window. Her soft feather bed enveloped her in caressing comfort, beckoning her to stay. Her sleepy mind drifted back to the handsome stranger. He was waving for her to join him. She was drawn to him as to a warm fire on a cold night. He reached down with his long, strong arms and scooped her up behind him on his horse. She clung to his powerful body. He wheeled his horse around and they rode west into the sunset.

"ALICE!!!" Her dream was interrupted again. "AL-I-C-E!!!" Mama's voice was drifting up the stairs. **"Ris' and shin', ve git vork to do!"**

Alice sat up in bed. She would rise, but she was not so sure about the shine part. After all, her romantic dream had just been doused with water. The fire was out.

"Alice, did ye hear me?"

"Yes, Mother! I'm coming!" Mama would say the faded, blue dress could be worn another day before washing, but Alice was sure she had spilled lemonade on it with a stomach of butterflies churning out of control. She took her brown dress off the peg and replaced it with her cotton nightgown. The dress was trimmed with a white collar and white cuffs on the sleeves. The brown print had tiny, white daisies. "He loves me, he loves me not, he loves me. NOT! Who would love a girl whose first appearance into the world was described as a crumpled walnut shell?" She was sure Papa and Mama were ready to marry her off, but with Papa's stories, all the suitors were sure to head for the hills. Alice looked into the mirror. "I'm doomed to be an old maid." Alice wished Mama had time to bob off her brown hair in the new *Roaring Twenties* style. This long hair was such a nuisance at times.

Alice braided her hair and wound it around her head, pinning it up in Norwegian style. Alice hurried down stairs and found a house full of company. Her older brother Jacob was feeding his two year old son some of his scrambled eggs. Ardis was sitting on Jacob's lap and mimicked everything his father did. His wife Edna sat next to him heavy with their next child. Across the table sat Alice's brother Elmer and his new wife Josephine. They had only been married a few months and were still enduring Papa's newlywed jokes. Mama was refilling the coffee cups.
"What are you doing here?" asked Alice.
Jacob answered, "Doing your chores, sleepyhead!"
"Slepehed," said Ardis putting his little hand on the top of his head.
"Heem so smart," bragged Grandfather Ed.
Elmer loved to tease as much as Ed and asked, "Alice did the sandman paste your eyes shut last night?"
Alice paused to think of a good come-back. "The sandman is on vacation, so I just stuck my head in the sand like an ostrich."
Laughter erupted all around the table. Ardis giggled and clapped his little hands. His giggles were contagious.
"Alice, I'm supposed to be the comedian of the family," chuckled Elmer. "I have to give it to you, Alice. You have always been quick-witted!"
Ed interrupted, "Not last nite. Alice vas al' tong'-tied."
Here we go again, thought Alice. She wished Papa would learn to bridle his tongue. His humiliating stories were a real source of irritation like a festering sliver under the skin. If Elmer got wind of this, she would never hear the end of it. Alice was giving Papa the evil eye when Mama jumped in. "Ja, Alice burnt da lefse, cuz she vas makin' kow eyes at dat goodt lukin' stranjer."
"Alice have you been holding out on me?" asked Elmer. "Makin' cow eyes, really Alice. You have got the love fever bad!" Elmer felt like he had hit a gold mine. He could now turn all this newlywed harassment around. He was glad to share the attention with Alice. "So you have a new beau? Well tell me, who is this good lookin' stranger who likes burnt lefse?"
"We did not feed him burnt lefse!" slammed Alice.
"You are avoiding my questions."
"Okay, we did have a handsome guest last night, but he is not interested in me."
Elmer gave Alice his evil grin. "By any chance will he be here, today?"

"Elmer, promise you will not embarrass me," begged Alice. "That is Father's specialty." Alice knew it was time to change the subject. "Father, did Dolly have her calf last night?"

"Not yet, but I fir if she gits ane big'er she von't fit thru da barn door. I sez ane tim', she 'bout rede."

"Amen to that," sighed Edna. "I do believe, I'm passed ready!"

That brought on more laughter and more clapping from little Ardis.

"Uffda, such karrein' on," laughed Tobia rising from the table. "Ve bet'er git a start on da pies."

Every one rose and followed her to the kitchen.

"Ve git da hot vater boilin'. How mane shickens ye need?" asked Ed.

"Fo'r vil' do. Nei, ye men eat lik' hors's. Bet'er kil' fiv'."

Alice, remembering her morning wake-up-call piped up, "Why not make it an even six? Don't you think it's about time to add Henry to the pot?"

"I'd like to get even," said Jacob. "I got bushwhacked by that old rooster trying to gather the eggs this morning. The old devil pecked me in the calf."

"He ain't no goodt fer fryin', too touf," said Tobia shaking her head. Then she started handing out orders. "Alice knead da bread an' git in pans. Edna an' Josie kin ye vork on da pies?"

Alice turned the sourdough unto the pastry board. It was made from starter, so they never had to buy yeast. Whenever they used a cup of starter, they fed the remainder with sugar and mashed potatoes. The starter churned and bubbled and multiplied. Alice loved to make bread. It fascinated her the way a small lump of dough could expand into a huge mass. After kneading the dough, she divided it into three pieces and placed them in the greased pans on the back of the cook-stove. She covered them with a clean dish towel as Tobia handed her the cookie recipes.

"Alice mak' a batch of jinjersnaps an' yus da rest of da razens to mak' som' o'tmeal kukes."

Then they heard an ear-splitting whistle bursting from Palmer's big steam tractor. **"Whooo-whooo!"**

Alice peeked out the kitchen window. The tractor was puffing along with its big iron wheels, towing the threshing machine. Dust was rising as wagons followed it into the yard.

"The threshers are coming!" announced Alice with excitement.

She saw Elmer running to open the pasture gate to let the big rig pass through followed by the horses and the wagons full of big, strong men.

Beyond the pasture lay the wheat field where Alice and Ed had built golden shocks of wheat from the bound sheaves produced by Ed's McCormick reaper. They had worked all week to be ready for this day, carefully spacing the shocks far enough apart so the wagons could pull up to them. The last wagon in the parade stopped at the house. A tall, handsome man jumped down and helped his petite wife down. She held on to the small mound of her unborn child. He reached into the wagon box and carried a wooden crate to the house. Tobia hurried to the porch and flung open the screen door.

"Velkommen til vart hjem!"

"Thank you, Mrs. Hoversten. My name is Walter Carson. I'm one of Palmer's friends. This is my wife Mary. She's come to help you feed the threshers."

"Com' in, dear. Hape to meet ye, Mary. Mor' hands litens da load."

"I made two pies," said Mary in her meek little voice.

Walter set down the crate of sweet corn. He handed the pies sitting on top, one to Mary and the other to Tobia.

"One is rhubarb and the other apple," explained Mary.

"Oh, dese vil' go nic'ly vith da blakbere pies Edna and Josie aur vorking on."

They heard a shrill **"Whoop, whoop, whoop!"** Palmer's tractor signaled the men were hard at work. Walter bent over and kissed Mary. "I can see you are in good company. I'll see you ladies at noon." Then he jumped up on the wagon seat, clucked to the horses and hurried toward the wheat field.

Ed hitched up his team and headed the two miles to the Thompson Creamery with the morning milk. Tobia had instructed him to stop at the General Store and get a sack of sugar, two pounds of coffee and a block of ice.

Jacob came in the house carrying Ardis who had fallen asleep on the porch next to the dog.

Elmer came in with the five chickens. They were cut up and ready for the frying pan.

Elmer teased, "What's all this cackling in here? For a moment, I thought I was in the hen house."

Tobia said, "I ges I not vorkin' ye hard enof Elmer. I se' ye stil' got spunk to tease da ladies. Go git bukit of vater fram da well. An' vhere is mi taters ye vas s'pos' to dig?"

"I set them on the porch," reported Jacob as he returned to the kitchen. He reached for some cookie dough and Tobia slapped him on the wrist.

"Nothing ever did get by your eagle eyes Mother," complained Jacob.
"Ye boys, sta' out of dat kuke dough or I vill slap ye sille!" ordered Tobia.
Elmer was eyeing his pretty wife. "I can't do another ounce of work until I get a kiss from my new bride." Then Elmer reached for Josie and devoured her lips.
"Ve, not hav' tim' fer tis foolishnes'. Ye boys git outsid'!" Tobia was waving her dish towel and shooing her sons out the door like she would chickens. She hollered after them, "Go vork in da veat field an' do not com' bak 'till I ring da din'er bell!" Tobia continued with the orders. "Alice an' Mary, hure an' git dose kukes in da oven. Ven dey com' out, da pies go in. Ven the pies com' out, da bre'd go in. I vill start fryin' shicken." Tobia took a big breath. When the last pan of cookies was out of the oven. Alice went to get the potatoes on the porch.
"I'll peel those," volunteered Edna. "I need to sit down and take a load off these aching feet."
Josie and Mary went out on the porch to shuck the corn.
"Alice, put dose kukes in a baskit an' tak' dem to da veat field. An' hure to feed dem hungre men lest dey starv'."
"Yes, Mother." Alice piled the gingersnaps on one side of the basket and the oatmeal raisin cookies on the other side. She carefully covered them with a clean dish towel to keep the flies at bay. With her Sunday-best white bonnet on her head and the basket of cookies on her arm, she headed for the wheat field.

~~~~~~

The sun was high in the sky. The men had worked at a steady pace all morning. When it came to threshing there was no time for slackers. Threshing was hard work and Palmer knew the men were tired, hungry and thirsty. He shut down the threshing machine and hollered, **"Let's take a break! Everyone stop and get a drink!"**
Jacob and Elmer had brought a cream can full of water from the well. They pried off the lid and handed the water dipper to Palmer's hired man, Oscar who was first in line. Oscar started on his third dipper when Jake gave him the elbow.
"There's a whole herd of camels behind you."
Oscar reluctantly handed the dipper to Jake and moved to the end of the

line.

Jake Anderson had leathery skin from many years in the sun. His dark hair was streaked with silvery gray, but he still claimed he could out work the young boys. He had a deep baritone voice and loved to sing. He believed the antidote for hard work was a song. Jake wiped his mouth with his sleeve and handed the dipper to Olaf.

Olaf Hanson was a strapping young fellow in his early twenties with sandy brown hair. He earned the nickname Plowboy.

"I sure am getting hungry, how about you Eli?" asked Olaf.

Eli answered, "hungry enough to eat a grizzly bear!" Eli Olafsen was a tall, sturdy man. Eli had a long, solid looking face with merry blue eyes. He had massive broad shoulders, arms bulging with sinewy muscles, big calloused hands, which wreaked havoc with anything that got in his way. He was a man with overwhelming strength and extraordinary endurance, yet his heart matched his size. Eli handed the dipper to Hans Peterson.

"Did you leave me any?" asked Hans.

"A few drops," answered Eli with a big grin on his face.

Hans had sparkling green eyes, fair skin, a freckled face and his shaggy red hair gave him a wild-look. His threshing buddies often called him, "The Fox."

"It's still cold," said Hans as he handed the dipper to Bjorn.

Bjorn Livingston was tall and had a rough looking appearance with ruddy cheeks and stormy gray eyes, but he was warm-hearted and good-natured.

"Walter it's all yours," said Bjorn handing over the water dipper.

Walter Carson was Palmer's loyal friend. He was quick on his feet and always ready to give a helping hand. Walter had a sunny disposition and always made the best out of every situation.

Palmer offered the dipper to the Hoversten brothers, but they insisted that he drink first.

Oscar interrupted the silence, "Well lookee at dat! I vonder vat she's got in dat dere baskit?"

Oscar was a stout man with a bull neck in his late forties. He loved to eat and it was starting to show.

The threshing crew turned to gawk at Alice coming across the wheat field. It was a breath catching moment!

Eli spoke first, "Well glory be..."

Olaf finished Eli's sentence. "Ain't dat a purte pic-sure!"

"She sur' is a comely lass." agreed Bjorn.

"Does anyone know her name?" asked Hans.

Jacob and Elmer looked at each other and smiled. They shrugged their shoulders like they didn't have a clue.

"I don't know," announced Olaf, "but I aim to find out."

Jake broke out in song, *"You are my sunshine, my only sunshine. You make me happy when skies are gray. You'll never know dear how much I love you, please don't take my sunshine away."*

It was difficult for the men to keep their eyes off this rare and lovely flower in the middle of a barren wheat field. Alice was a glowing vision, a ray of sunshine on a cloudy day. The sun shone on her delicate face framed in her white sunbonnet. She walked with the perfect symmetry of a precious flower gently moving in the breeze. The full skirt of her pretty dress with the tiny white daisies swirled around her legs as she walked. Her graceful movements were like fluttering, white butterflies, twisting and turning, rising and falling.

Palmer's heart skipped like a child going out to play.

Elmer looked at Jacob. "Are you thinking what I'm thinking?"

Jacob answered, "Ja, that basket is full of cookies."

Elmer shouted, "Last one's a rotten egg!" as he took off running to meet Alice.

Jacob followed at his heels. After getting slapped for stealing cookie dough, he was determined to get the first cookie.

"My, you boys must be starving," giggled Alice handing over the cookies. "Make sure you don't eat the basket." Then she turned around and headed back to the house.

Elmer lifted the towel and Jacob grabbed an oatmeal cookie. "I suppose we have to share," complained Elmer.

"If ye dun't, Mother vill slap ye sille," said Jacob mimicking Tobia's voice.

Walter nudged Palmer. "She's very charming," he whispered. "It's not every day you find a flower in a wheat field. It's time to pick this one before someone else does."

Palmer knew Walter was right. His heart had melted last night when he had looked into Alice's big, brown eyes. Since then, he could think of nothing else. But he wondered was he reaching for a flower that would always be just beyond his grasp? The very thought gave him a rainy-day feeling with dark clouds blocking out his sunshine. The one thing he was sure of, he had met the love of his life. But did this delicate, rare flower feel the same way?

Palmer watched the delicate flower leave the wheat field, like the morning mist that quickly vanishes with the rising sun.

Chapter 3   The Dinner Bell

The sun was straight over head and Palmer knew it was almost noon. He shut down the tractor.
"Let's unhitch the horses," he hollered. **"They need a rest!"**
"There's a horse trough by the windmill," offered Jacob.
They were leading the horses across the pasture when they heard the dinner bell, **"Dong, dong, dong!"**
   "Dat's a velcom' sound," huffed Oscar as he struggled to keep up.
"You guys go ahead. Jacob and I will take care of the horses," volunteered Elmer.
The threshers hurried to the water pump like tired camels to a refreshing oasis.
Ed had made a table with two saw horses and a wide board. He had set out washbasins, bars of soap, a pile of flour-sack towels and filled two milk pails and a wooded bucket with clean water.
The men doffed their hats in a pile and started washing the dirt and sweat off their faces, arms and hands. Eli stuck his head under the pump and doused himself with the cool well water. Others eagerly waited for their turn.
Ed came out on the porch and hollered, "Din'er rede! I reckon y'r all 'bout gon' fer hunger. C'mon in!"
The smell of fresh baked bread drew the men into the house like a magnet.
"Velkommen til vart hjem!" announced Tobia forgetting her English as she led the way to the dining room.
Ed and Alice had extended the table to threshing size by adding all the table leaves. They had hunted down every chair, stool, bench and barrel on the farm for seating. The women were busy bringing food and drinks to the table.
Oscar chose a seat next to the dutch oven of fried chicken. He picked up his fork ready to stab a drum stick, when Ed announced, "Let us giv' takks."
Heads bowed all around the table like falling dominoes.
"Heavenly Fader, Allmekliage Gud, it is vith great rejoicing dat ve com' to ye, today. Ye hav' blessed us vith plentiful rain an' sunshin' an' now ve hav' a fin' veat crop. Ve takk ye fer dese strong, hardt vorking men who bring in da harvest. Ve takk ye fer da lovin' hands of dese vomen who prepar' dis harvest feast fer us. But most of al', ve takk you fer sendin' y'r only begotten

Son to die fer us so dat ve may live. It is in Jesus nam' dat ve pray. Amen." Amens echoed all around the table.

"Let's eat men!" said Ed has he reached for the bowl of mashed potatoes with gusto.

Oscar still with fork in hand stabbed at the chicken, faster than a goose chasing after a June bug! The men filled their plates to overflowing. Alice brought in fresh, churned butter for the sweet corn and sourdough bread. She added jars of strawberry jam, grape jelly and a small crock of golden honey to the collection. She caught Palmer's gaze and smiled. The butterflies in her stomach started fluttering out of control. Palmer's eyes followed Alice each time she left the room and each time she returned. He wanted to look into her big, brown eyes, but she was always darting away. It seemed the more he looked at her; he only wanted to look more.

"Alice, I hope ye made plente food," mumbled Oscar with a full mouth. "Eli has two hollow legs."

"It's better to have hollow legs than a hollow head," slammed Eli. Laughter erupted from around the table.

Alice returned with a big bowl of creamy, sweet coleslaw. She stole a glance at Palmer and their eyes met. Alice felt she might drown in his gaze.

Palmer's heart leaped as Alice approached. Her eyes held him captive. Palmer knew he was completely smitten. His smile blazed like the glorious sunrise bursting above the horizon.

As good as the food was, Palmer still had trouble concentrating on the meal. Alice was beautiful! Her braided hair was wrapped around her head like a crown. He was sure she was prettier than any princess had ever been.

Ed interrupted Palmer's thoughts breaking the spell, "Is dat y'r fader who runs da blacksmith shop?"

Palmer answered; "Yes." his mind was still on Alice.

"I thout so, same last nam' as y'rs," chuckled Ed. "He fix vagon vhe'l fer me an' do a goodt job!"

Jake asked, "Did Mr. Ellwood bring his stallion in? I have a couple of mares that need to be serviced."

Palmer answered, "Ja, he's in that pen behind the livery stable."

Eli worked at the Blacksmith Shop and he joined the conversation. "That stallion is a mean old brute! I'd like to yank his teeth out. Andrew Serby's pony got loose and that stallion took a big chunk of hide out of the pony's shoulder. Doc said the pony might not make it."

Oscar interrupted, "Kin ye pass me dose taters?"
Jake handed what was left of the potatoes to Oscar and asked, "Do you know how much Mr. Ellwood charges for the stallion's service?"
Eli answered, "You'll have to take that up with him."
Ed started in with one of his stories. "I got da job dun free! Gunvor Torgeson's bul' yump da fenc' and git in vith mi cows. Gunvor vas in town askin' if anevon' se' his bul'. I yust vait 'til' bul' finish his vork, den I ask Gunvor if heem 'no' anevon' missin' a Holstein bul'. Ja, dey is rit, Amarika da land of da free!"
The threshing crew bellowed with laughter.
Ed continued, "I git al' heifer calves out of dat bul'. Goodt bul'! He dun't 'no' how to mak' bul' calves."
Laughter shook the house.
When the roaring died down Ed added, "Ja, I sur' hope dat bul' yump da fence ag'in vhen I need heem."
Another round of laughter rocked the house.
Oscar asked, "Anyon' goin' to eat dat last ros'n ear?"
"Where you puttin' all that food, Oscar?" asked Jake. "You are the one with two hollow legs!"
Olaf teased, "He'll be splittin' out his britches again."
"Oscar, I sure hope you have drawers on this time!" exclaimed Hans.
"Aur ye men rede fer pie?" asked Tobia.
"I thought you'd never ask," said Elmer.
"Mother what kind do you have?" asked Jacob.
"Mary mad' r'ubarb an' appl' an' y'r vives mad' blakbere, too."
Eli interrupted, "Mrs. Hoversten, I see you have a treadle sewing machine. "Are you a seamstress?"
"Dat vud be mi Alice. Dat gerl sews lik' a hum'in'bird."
Alice entered the dining room with a pie in each hand.
"Miss Alice, how 'bout I give you my threshing check in exchange for some new shirts," pleaded Eli.
"I would love to sew you some new shirts, but you'll only have to pay for the fabric and thread." Alice's soft voice felt musical to Palmer's ears.
"Oh, no, Miss Alice! Eli Olafsen pays his way. Palmer pays me well and I have a check from the Blacksmith Shop, too. You sew, I pay!"
Alice opened the top drawer of the sewing machine cabinet. " I'll have to get your measurements." She took out a scrap of paper, a pencil and a

paper measuring tape.

Eli stood up towering over Alice. "I smell pretty bad, Miss Alice!"

"Ye kin sez dat ag'in," mumbled Oscar with his mouth full of apple pie.

"Maybe, you'll want to measure in the morning after I take a bath."

"I think you already had a bath at the pump," giggled Alice. "Your shirt is still wet." Alice stretched up on her tiptoes to measure Eli's chest.

"Ja, I'm like a big child when it comes to splashin' in water!"

Jake asked, "Alice do you know how to measure in horse hands? He's big as a horse! Mr. Ellwood's stallion is no match for Eli."

Muffled snickering came from the stuffed mouths of the threshing crew!

Olaf added, "Eli could hold that stallion down with his thumb!"

Eli's threshing buddies had their mouths so full of pie, they could only smile and grunt.

"Save me some of that pie you vultures!" exclaimed Eli.

Alice thought Eli certainly did need a new shirt. This one was not only threadbare, but peppered with burn holes from his blacksmith job. It wouldn't even make a good rag. The sleeves were already ripped to his armpits. Alice wondered how it held together at all.

Hans piped up, "It's hard to keep muscles like that corralled."

"Ja, they are bound to bust out like a wild stallion!" laughed Elmer.

Laughter burst forth at the table!

"How long?" asked Alice.

"I want it extra-long. It always comes out of my trousers and can you make the sleeves a little bigger. They always rip out!"

"I wonder why?" spouted Bjorn and more snickering came from the threshing crew.

Alice asked, "What's your favorite color, Eli?"

Eli got a big grin on his face and said, "That would be blue."

"I should have known!" smiled Alice.

"I'd take a brown shirt if it was as pretty as your big, brown eyes, Miss Alice."

Like the tide rushing in, Palmer's mind was overtaken by a tormenting thought. *What if Alice is in love with Eli?* His heart capsized driven like a rudderless ship at sea. His emotions were whirling him about, sucking him under. He wished he was wearing Eli's shoes right now, standing there staring into Alice's brown eyes. But would a beautiful woman like Alice give him a second glance? Was there even the tiniest flicker of hope? Walter gave Palmer a sympathetic glance. He noticed Palmer's face was a mask of concern.

"Eli, you are so kind," Alice replied softly. "I'll see what I can find. I know they have some new bolts of fabric at the General Store. Any long sleeve shirts?"

"Better get a few."

Alice measured from Eli's shoulder to his wrist and wrote the total inches on her paper. "Just one more Eli. Can you bend down, so I can measure your neck?"

"She'll need a ladder to reach the top!" smirked Hans.

Oscar interrupted again, "Is dere ane mor' r'ubarb pie? I ain't tried dat von yet."

"Oscar you touch that last piece of pie and I'll hang you out to dry!" warned Eli.

Were the men choking on laughter or pie?

"Uffda!" exclaimed Tobia. "Ye men keep karrein' on and ye all split y'r britches. Alice be up al' nite sewin'!

Walter sensing Palmer's heart ache replied, "I think it's about time for us to get back to work. You boys will be all tuckered out from laughing."

Palmer agreed, "Mrs. Hoversten, everything was absolutely delicious. We appreciate your generous hospitality!"

"Mange Takk! Ye aur velkommen, Mr. Helgren.

"I do apologize for the men eating like Clydesdales!"

Ed chuckled, "Da men vork hardt! Ye 'no' vot da goodt book sez, 'ye must not muzzle da ox ven heem is thrashin' da veat.'"

Chapter 4 The Bet

Eli followed the men outside ducking under the door frame. "If I had eaten one more morsel, I'd be stuck in the doorway!"
"We could always pull you out with Palmer's tractor," laughed Olaf.
Oscar wormed his way through the men and took off running for the outhouse.
"I've never seen Oscar move so fast!" exclaimed Walter.
"Bet he's got the runs again," chuckled Bjorn.
"It serves him right," said Palmer. "He ate a bushel basket of food!"
"I goin' to da veat field," announced Ed. "I kin't vork lik' ye youn' felos, but I kin stil' driv' da vagon. Ol' ag' kechin' up vith me. How ye Amarikans sez... 'I ain't vorth a plug nikel anemor'?"
The threshing crew struck out for the field and Jake broke out in song, *"Ooo, the ol' gray mare she ain't what she used to be,"*-the others joined in-*"ain't what she used to be, ain't what she used to be. The ol' gray mare she ain't what she used to be, many long years ago..."*

~~~~~~

Little Ardis walked around the table, assessing the situation. "Big mess! Big mess!" he said shaking his little head. He climbed up on a chair and reported, "Mommy, dey ate al' da taters!"
"Get down before you break your crown!" demanded Edna.
Ardis sang, *"Jack fell down an' broke his crown* an' Jill fell down the hill, too. Didn't she Mommy?"
"Yes, she did," answered Edna "and that's why I want you to get down!"
Tobia put a kettle of water on the stove and Alice headed for the pump to get more water. Edna, Josie and Mary brought the dirty dishes to the kitchen followed by Ardis proudly carrying the spoons. Alice poured water into the dry-sink and added hot water from the kettle.
"I'll wash," volunteered Mary.
Tobia handed flour-sack towels to Edna and Josie. "Alice, ye bet'er bake som' more kukes," suggested Tobia. "Ve've got sour kream in da ic' box."
"Grandmother Enga's sour cream cookies, that's Father's favorite."
"Ja," Tobia's voice trembled. "Bet'er dubel Moder's resipe if ve got enof kream."
Memories of Norway flooded Tobia's mind and fresh tears forged a trail down her cheeks.

"Mother are you okay?" Alice asked gently.

"I 'member da day ve left aur hom'land." Tobia's voice cracked. "Ve not vant to leav', but dere's not enof land. So ve aur forc'd to go avay." Tobia's words came raspy. "Ve felt lik' fish kech't in dragnet. I se' Edward's folks, Jacob an' Anna, wavin'. Fader an' Moder standin' dere, too," her voice quivered. "An' I 'no' I never se' ag'in." Tears streamed down Tobia's face like the tide racing in.

Alice wrapped her arms around Tobia, "Oh, Mother, you are the bravest one I know. What you did was so very hard to do!"

Josie said with sympathy, "To come to a new land, learn a new culture, a new language that would overwhelm anyone."

"I'm so glad you came to America. Tobia you are the best mother-in-law ever," added Edna.

"To leave family behind, that took great courage," Mary replied softly.

"Nei, I vas not brav'," Tobia's voice carried sadness. "I vept so much, flood da oshen, 'most drown da fish."

Then everyone burst into laughter and the dark cloud that had invaded Tobia's mind evaporated.

Little Ardis clapped his hands. "Be hape, gamma!"

Tobia picked him up and kissed him on the cheek. "Vho not hape vith ye araund?"

"I make you cookie. Then you be hape. Me big boy, me kin help," pleaded Ardis looking at Alice.

"Okay, Ardis you can stir for Auntie Alice."

Tobia set him next to the bowl and handed Ardis her big wooden spoon.

"I like cookies, Ante Alice."

"Father like son," added Edna as she dried another plate.

Alice whispered to Ardis. "Ye better not become a cookie dough thief. Gamma Tobia vill slap ye silly!" Then Ardis and Alice got the giggles!

"What's so funny?" asked Josie.

Ardis answered with a big grin, "It's a secret, kin't tell." Alice filled the oven with cookies. "Mother can you watch the cookies while I go get more wood?"

"Ja, tak' out da dish vater vhen ye go."

"I open door," offered Ardis pushing open the screen door.

Alice was glad to be outside. It was stifling hot in the kitchen! The cook-stove had been stoked since dawn. Ardis followed Alice like a shadow to the woodpile. Alice gathered a bundle of oak and locust which was preferred for baking. She handed a small piece of hickory to Ardis.

"Ante Alice, I'm a big boy," his little face beamed with pride.

"You are so big! The best helper I've ever had."
Mary saw them coming and swung open the screen door. "I see you have a little helper."
"I'm strong lik' Dadde," said Ardis.
Josie announced, "We are headed to the garden to pick green beans and we could sure use a strong man."
"I can pick beans," reported Ardis.
"Good! Put your stick in the wood box and come help us," suggested Edna.

~~~~~~

The men were hard at work by the time Oscar reached the wheat field. It was a hot day and Oscar was sweating profusely from the walk. He headed straight for the cream can and started guzzling his fill of water. He took his straw hat off and poured the cool, refreshing water over his head. It felt wonderful! He poured a second and then a third dipper over his head until water ran off his walrus mustache. He took out his handkerchief and threw it in the cream can soaking up every drop. He wrapped the cool hanky around his neck and smiled with a sinister grin. He would blame the water shortage on Eli. It was much too hot to be threshing wheat reasoned Oscar. Besides he had eaten too much dinner and now he was sleepy. The men were so busy, no one would miss him. He crept behind a wheat shock and laid down for a nap.
Palmer was throwing another shovel of coal into the fire box on the tractor, when he saw Oscar disappear behind a wheat shock.
"What's he doing over there?" mumbled Palmer.
Everyone knew that Oscar had a lackadaisical attitude when it came to work. Too bad he didn't feel the same about food. Palmer took off his hat, wiped the sweat from his face with his sleeve and headed for the cream can. The ground around the can was wet, really wet. He took off the lid and peered inside. It was just what he had suspected, bone dry. Palmer knew Oscar had taken a bath with their precious drinking water. *How could Oscar be so thoughtless about the needs of others?* He headed straight for the wheat shock that he had seen Oscar sneak behind.
Palmer kicked Oscar's boot. "Get up!"
Oscar struggled to sit up.
"Get the cream can and go get us some water!" ordered Palmer.
Oscar slowly got to his feet teetering a moment before regaining his balance. *How did Palmer find him? He was sure no one had seen him.* "Do I hafta? Why dun't ye hav' Eli do it?"

"Eli's working! You Oscar are the new water-boy. Now get going!" Palmer's voice carried a tone of finality.

"Dat kre'm kin too heav' to kave dat far! Kin I yus a vagon?"

"All the wagons are in use. You've got a half hour to get back here and that cream can better be full to the brim!"

"Nei!" Bold as brass, Oscar protested. "I ain't, I ain't gonna do it!"

Rumor was that Oscar's mental processes were a little slow. Palmer didn't put much stock in rumors, but Oscar was certainly proving this one true. Palmer shook his head and started walking away. "Oscar you better look for a new job!"

"Aw, shucks, I vas yust joshn', goin' rit now! DID YE HEAR ME? RIT NOW! PALMER I BE RIT BACK!" hollered Oscar.

~~~~~~

"It so hot in da kitshun," said Tobia fanning herself with her apron. "I 'bout burnt up!"

"Why don't you sit down under the shade tree Mother?" suggested Alice. "You need to cool down."

"Ye gerls giv' me som' of dose beans an' I kin start snappin'."

Ardis had picked three beans and dropped them into his mother's pail. But now he was chasing a yellow butterfly. Whenever it landed on the beans, he tiptoed closer, but when he grabbed for it the butterfly always moved out of reach.

Edna had turned over a bucket for a chair. The heaviness of her womb made squatting for very long intolerable. Everytime she moved her bucket, she rubbed her aching back trying to get the kinks out.

"When is your baby due?" asked Mary.

Edna answered, "In a few weeks. I'm so hot and miserable, I can't wait! When are you expecting?"

"Our blessed event will occur in the fall." said Mary. "Walter can't wait either. He rubs my belly every day and talks to the baby as if it is already here."

Oscar interrupted, startling the women. "Ye got a vhelbaro? I got to tak' vater to da field."

"Dere's von in da barn dat ye kin yus," offered Tobia.

"Takk!" Oscar ambled toward the barn.

Alice wondered how well Mary knew Palmer. How could she ask questions without letting everyone know she was interested in him? Yet she wanted to know more. Josie came to her rescue when she asked, "How long have you known Mr. Helgren?"

Mary answered, "Walter and Palmer are very good friends. Palmer was our best man at our wedding last summer. He's a wonderful neighbor. Whenever we need help he's the first one there."

Edna joined the conversation. "Palmer's a very handsome man. I'm surprised he doesn't have a wife. Is he courting anyone?"

"He sets all the girls in a flutter," giggled Mary.

Alice knew that was true. Whenever she gazed into those sky-blue eyes her butterflies fluttered out of control.

Mary continued, "I guess Palmer hasn't found the right one yet. He works so hard, I don't think he has time for a wife."

Tobia jumped in. "He need a goodt voman dat 'no' how to kuk. He is vay too thin!"

Oscar interrupted again, "Kin I git a helpin' hand?"

Alice jumped up and met Oscar at the pump. Josie saw them struggling with the cream can and came to the rescue.

"Whew! Dat sur' is heave!" complained Oscar.

"Are you going to be able to get that to the field?" questioned Alice.

"Ayup! I usin' my head dis tim'. I yust vheel it down dere," bragged Oscar as he wobbled off with his heavy load.

Alice gave the women a wary look. "I sure hope he doesn't hit a pot-hole and turn that cream can topsy-turvy!"

Josie giggled, "Imagine Oscar racing down the hill chased by a cream can!"

The garden was filled with laughter and little Ardis clapped his hands.

Alice had built up the courage to ask Mary a question. "Did Palmer's folks come from Sweden?"

"His father John was born in Ystad, Sweden. He came to America when he was nineteen. But Palmer's mother Martha was born near Decorah, Iowa."

"Ve thout he vas a Swede. Dat blon' hair an' blu' eyes giv' heem avay. I tel' Alice he is a goodt kech, just lik' her Fader. Bet'er snag heem quick lest he get avay!" advised Tobia looking at Alice.

"Mother, he's not a fish," replied Alice with blushing cheeks.

"Takk goodness! Ye ain't a vere goodt fish'rman," said Tobia adding her sweet chuckle. "Mary do you com' fram a big famle?"

"Just two sisters, Malena and I are twins. You might know my older sister Rachel. She's the mid-wife."

"Rachel Allison is your sister?" queried Edna. "She was so helpful when I had Ardis. Rachel is very good at what she does."

Mary explained, "My mother was a mid-wife. She always took Rachel with her. Mother claimed it was Rachel's calling. She was blessed with those long, slender hands and could always turn the breach babies on the first try."

Edna gave Mary a quizzical look. "I would have never thought you were sisters. Rachel is so tall. How did that happen?"

Mary hesitated not knowing how to respond. "Life doesn't always deal a fair hand. I got robbed! Rachel got Father's long legs and Malena and I inherited Mother's short legs." Mary tried to stifle her giggles. "Mother always said, 'You get what you get and you don't throw a fit!'"

A grin split Tobia's face. "Dose short legs vork da same as da long vons do."

~~~~~~

The men saw Oscar coming with the wheelbarrow. Palmer shut down the threshing machine and the men congregated to get a drink. Oscar staggered to a stop with his heavy load. "I dun't spill a drop," he huffed.

"Why are you huffing and puffing like a freight train?" inquired Jake.

"Oof! Dat's so heave ye kin't even lift it!"

"How did you get it in the wheelbarrow?" asked Palmer.

"Um...ah," Oscar cleared his throat. "Da vomen-folk giv' helpin' han'."

"Sounds like the women did all the work, so what are you moaning about?" teased Hans.

Oscar held up his hand, "Lookee I git blister!"

"Ooh, do you want me to kiss your boo-boo?" mocked Bjorn.

Walter snickered, "A little spit oughta fix that, don't you think Oscar?"

"It ain't funne! It 'mos' kil' me gettin' dat kin down here," whined Oscar.

"I would have carried it from the well without all this caterwaulin!" scoffed Eli.

"I bet ye a ten dol'ar bil' ye kin't kave dat kin to da well an' back!" spouted Oscar.

Eli with the light of battle in his eyes exclaimed, "I'll take you up on that bet! Ten dollars sez I can!"

"In a pig's eye! Ye kin't do it ye big ol' ox!"

Eli reached for the cream can grabbing it by one handle and swung it up onto his shoulder. He started for the well.

Enthusiasm stirred up like a fire and whoops of glee came from the threshing crew as they followed Eli.

"I not hav' dis much fun in a long tim'!" chuckled Ed.

"Me either," added Elmer.

"That's not true," laughed Jacob. "He's a newlywed."
"Just tryin' to keep up with my big brother," laughed Elmer giving Jacob a hearty slap on the back.
"Ye kin't set dat kin down!" yelled Oscar. "Got to kave to well an' back vithout settin' down! YE HEAR ME ELI!"
Olaf ran ahead to open the pasture gate and Eli strutted through with his heavy load. Olaf turned to the threshers and shouted, "Look at him go! Eli's burnin' back the wind!"
"Votda ye dink?" croaked Oscar with a worried tone. "He ain't gonna mak' it, is he?"
"I don't think he's even tapped into his second wind," laughed Jake. "I can barely keep up with him!"
The noisy high spirits of the threshing crew spurred Eli on!

~~~~~~

"Listen, I hear voices," remarked Alice.
"Me too!" shouted Ardis.
"Takk goodtness! I thout I los' mi mind," sighed Tobia with relief.
Alice rose and shielded her eyes with her hand looking into the sun. "It's the men! Why are they coming up to the house?"
"What on earth is going on?" asked Josie getting up.
Mary asked, "Do you think someone is hurt?"
"I told Edward to sta' out of da sun," cried Tobia. "He never listen!"
"Isn't that Eli in the lead?" asked Edna waddling up behind them.
"Ja, and he's carrying that heavy cream can!" exclaimed Alice.
"Dose men ain't got a lick of sense," said Tobia joining the group.
Ardis clapped his hands. It looked like a race and Daddy was in it. "Horsey-ride," he cried and ran toward Jacob to hop on board.
Eli made a beeline straight for the pump, slapped the top and headed back to the wheat field trudging along with bulldog tenacity.
"Keep on truckin' Eli!" shouted Bjorn.
Hans chimed in, "Show those muscles whose boss!"
"Ve got a bet goin' on here!" hollered Ed to the women as he headed to the pump for a drink.
Tobia called to Palmer, "Ye ain't vorkin' dose men hardt enof if dey stil' got spunk fer gam's."
Palmer smiled, "I have to let them have a little fun once in a while."

"Ye a goodt man, Mr. Helgren," returned Tobia. "A goodt man!"

Alice stared in stunned silence. Palmer's captivating smile lit a fire in her heart. *This one was surely a keeper. Like always, Mama was right. Palmer was a very good catch! Alice was sure many fine ladies had cast a line at him. But he always got away. Alice wondered how she could reel him in.* Hope fluttered in her heart.

Mary asked her husband, "Who are you betting on?"

"Eli, of course! Oscar is sweatin' bullets with every step," chuckled Walter.

Elmer's eyes lit up with mischief, "I missed you, my love. Can I steal a kiss?"

"Get away Elmer!" Josie pushed him back with out-stretched arms. "You are all sweaty!"

Jacob galloped up with Ardis on his back. "Get this little buckaroo off my back. I've got to go back to work."

Alice lifted Ardis off. "Horsey-ride, Ante Alice, p'eas'!"

The men all jogged to catch up with Eli.

"Slow down Eli!" yelled Elmer. "We're gettin' winded back here!"

Oscar was starting to panic. He didn't have a dime to his name. He picked up a dried cow chip in the pasture and flung it at Eli. It hit Eli in the chest, but Eli didn't even flinch. Oscar grabbed another cow chip and fired it at Eli's back. It hit him between the shoulder blades, but Eli continued on at breakneck speed.

"Aw, now you've gone and done it," scolded Olaf.

"Oscar you are dumber then dirt," warned Bjorn. "Eli's goin' to make you eat those cow chips."

Oscar ignored the warning and bent over to pick up a whole cow pie.

Jake had caught a bull snake and flung it at Oscar to even the score.

Oscar let out a screech and scrambled to get away with anger smoldering in his eyes.

"Oscar you are jumpy as a rattlesnake," laughed Elmer.

Eli was starting across the wheat field and was now out of firing range.

"Buck up Eli, you can do it," cheered Hans.

Eli's muscles screamed in protest, but he kept right on truckin'.

"Ain't much farther," encouraged Olaf.

Bjorn ran ahead to the wheelbarrow and yelled, "You got this Eli! I smell ten bucks!"

"Better get your wallet out Oscar," shouted Walter.

Eli lifted the heavy burden off his shoulder and set it down in the wheelbarrow. He bellowed out a mighty roar, "Ya-hoo!" then stepped back, triumphant.

A great shout of praise came from the threshing crew. They were all stunned by the feat of strength they had just witnessed.

Oscar stood there with a dumbfounded look on his face and a scowl creased his forehead.

"Payday Oscar!" yelled Bjorn.

Eli popped the lid off and took a much deserved drink.

Hans shouted, "Divvy up, Oscar!"

"You lost Oscar, now it's time to pay up!" cried Olaf.

"Er-hrm, kin't, ain't got it," croaked Oscar.

"What do you mean, you ain't got it?" bellowed Eli.

"Ain't got it, I'm plumb broke," confessed Oscar. "Ain't got even a nickel."

Eli hollered, "Oscar you ain't no smarter than that ol' gray mare, we've been singing about! You don't bet money you don't have!"

Oscar stepped backwards. "Eli I dun't dink ye could do it!"

With adrenaline pumping, Eli leaped like a cougar, grabbing Oscar's ankles! He effortlessly flipped Oscar upside down and pumped him up and down like a yo-yo. Oscar struggled to get away, but Eli hung on to the squirming man with a steel like grip!

"Stop, stop!" howled Oscar. "I gitten' headak!" He thrashed around, but to no avail.

"Let me go, ye big brute!" Oscar's words came raspy.

"Oscar if you ever throw another cow chip at me, I'll stick your head in a fresh cow pie!" Eli threatened. "That bald head of yours will be wearin' a new crop of hair."

A titter of laughter came from the threshers. Then Eli dropped Oscar like a bulldogged steer.

Chapter 5   The Big Wooden Spoon

"I tink ve got enof beans to run da canner," sighed Tobia.
"And you have enough cucumbers to start a pickle factory!" declared Josie standing in the middle of the cucumber patch.
"I'll start washing up the canning jars," volunteered Edna.
"Ardis do you want to play hide-and-go-seek?" asked Alice.
"Yeah!" Ardis came skipping toward her.
"Mr. Zucchini is hiding under these leaves. See if you can find him."
Ardis squatted down and cautiously peeked under the mass of vines and leaves about to take over the garden. "I see 'im," he reported with excitement.. "How we get 'im out of dere?"
"You hold the leaves back and I'll twist him off." Alice spun the zucchini around until the stem broke. "This one was holding on for dear life! See if you can find one of his neighbors."
Mary was in the next row pulling up carrots. "You'll make a great mother someday, Alice."
"I'm going to take her to school with me, so she can entertain my students," piped up Josie.
"I'm afraid I'll be an old maid," cried Alice.
Ardis asked, "What is old maid?"
Alice explained, "It's a woman who never gets married."
"You kin marre me," offered Ardis.
"There would never be a dull moment with you around," giggled Alice.
Tobia stood up and wiped her brow with the corner of her apron. "Ve got kream. I vas dinking ve kud mak' som' ic' kream to go vith kukes."
Ardis jumped up and down clapping his hands.
"I'll go down the cellar and get the ice cream churn and the rock salt," volunteered Alice. "Then, I'm going to go check on Dolly. I saw her heading for the woods."
Josie added, "I'll go shave some ice off the block."
"I can help," offered Ardis.
"Good!" said Edna. "You can have a turn at running the crank."

~~~~~~

Alice headed towards a wooded area at the north end of the pasture. She knew Dolly would try to find a secluded place to have her calf. In a clearing behind a bunch of willow bushes, Alice found Dolly and her new twin calves. Dolly was busy licking her new babies. One was struggling to stand up and took a few wobbly steps only to fall back down. Dolly nudged the other calf who tried to stand on her trembling legs, but plunged right on top of her sister.

"C'mon girls keep trying," encouraged Alice. "You'll get the hang of it."

After several tries both calves were on their feet. Dolly swung her head and pushed the twins toward her udder. The hungry calves wasted no time finding their new food source. Alice could tell the calves were enjoying their first meal. Their little tails were swishing to and fro like a couple of pendulums. Dolly kept her tail moving too, switching away the biting flies. Alice gave the calves plenty of time to nurse. When she was satisfied that their tummies were full, Alice broke off a willow branch. She knew the new calves would be much safer in the barn. She tapped Dolly on the rump.

"C'mon Dolly, it's time to go home."

The disgruntled mama lowed and tossed her head warning Alice that she was still the boss. Then she ambled along slowly, stopping once in a while to make sure her calves were following.

Alice followed with a merry heart, knowing Papa would be overjoyed to be adding two more heifers to his dairy herd.

The women had set up their ice cream factory on the work table under the shade tree. Then they started the tedious job of continuous cranking. Soon they heard the jingle of a horse harness. The men were returning with wagons full of golden wheat followed by Palmer's tractor and threshing machine.

"Dose men got goodt timin' an' goodt noses, too," chuckled Tobia. "I dun't dink dey kud smel' ic' kream."

The women brought out bowls, spoons and the big basket full of Alice's sour cream cookies. Ardis followed carrying Grandmother Tobia's big, wooden spoon to scoop up the ice cream.

Elmer flopped down on the lawn for a nap.

"Are you men done?" asked Josie.

"Ja, we are s-o-o-o done!" exclaimed Elmer always joking around. "I'm done, put a fork in me."

"We might just do that," teased Josie. "We don't have anything ready for supper."

Ed and Palmer went up on the porch to settle up.

"Alice is mi sekretere. I hav' her mak' out check." Ed combed the yard and hollered, "Vher' is Alice?"
Edna laughed, "She had a marriage proposal today. Maybe, she eloped with Ardis."
"Nei, I still here!" called Ardis who crawled out from under the work table, where he patiently waited for ice cream.
Tobia answered, "Dolly mis'in' so Alice go luk fer her."
"How long as she been gone?" asked Jacob.
"Long enof to mak' me vorre," said Tobia with a weary voice.
"Did that good-for-nothing dog go along?" asked Elmer sitting up.
"Nei, he under porch," reported Ardis.
"That worthless old dog!" exclaimed Elmer getting to his feet.
Jacob questioned the women. "Did anyone see which way she went?"
"Vent north to da voods I dink," explained Tobia.
Palmer sprang to his feet. "I'll go look for her!"
The threshing crew all volunteered to help, except for Oscar, of course, who sat down next to the ice cream table.
Josie announced, "Quiet! I hear whistling."
"O my darlin' Clementine," remarked Jake identifying the tune.
Ed, from his vantage point on the porch hollered, "Here dey com' now!"
When Alice saw the crowd, she stopped whistling and waved her willow stick in the air.
Palmer breathed a sigh of relief. *Is there anything this beautiful woman can't do?*
When Alice was in earshot, Ed hollered, "Did ve git a heifer calf?"
"Nei," giggled Alice shaking her head. "We got **two** heifer calves!"
"I so proud, I 'bout to burst. I told ye boys dat vas a goodt bul'!" bragged Ed.
The men roared with laughter!
Palmer ran to open the barn yard gate and Alice herded the new family into the corral. Palmer gazed into Alice's shining eyes and spoke out of the tenderness of his heart. "Alice, you simply amaze me! I believe there's nothing you can't do!"
"I didn't do anything special," laughter peeked out around Alice's brown eyes. "Dolly did all the work. I know Father is very pleased."
"I think he's about ready to buy Gunvor Torgeson's Holstein bull. All heifers, that's remarkable. Plus a set of twins. Times like this are rare indeed!" exclaimed Palmer.
Ardis came skipping down to the barn yard to see the new calves. Palmer lifted him up so he could see over the fence.

"Are you goin' to marry my Ante Alice?" asked Ardis. "She mak' good cookies!"
"She sure does, but I heard you already proposed," laughed Palmer.
"Momme sez I kin't, cuz she is mi Ante," explained Ardis.
"That does propose quite a problem," said Palmer. "I'd like to help you out. Would you and Auntie Alice like to go on a picnic with me, so we can get to know each other a little better?"
"Kin we Ante Alice?" begged Ardis.
"Sure, I love picnics!"
"Well, it's a date then," smiled Palmer.
"Horsey ride, p'eas'!" begged Ardis climbing onto Palmer's back.
"I think you have a new friend," giggled Alice.
"C'mon ve selebrat' vith ic' kream an' kukes!!!" shouted Ed from the porch.
"Giddy up!" cried Ardis.
"Let's go see if they saved us some ice cream," came Alice's sweet voice.
Palmer laughed, "The odds are against us with Oscar around."
Ardis reported, "Gamma got BIG spoon!"
"There's hope," giggled Alice. "Nothing gets past Mother's big wooden spoon!"

Chapter 6   Tin Lizzie

The threshing crew had just finished licking their ice cream bowls when the silence was shattered, **"Oogah! Oogah!"** A shiny black motorcar was cruising up the Hoversten lane blasting the Klaxon.
"Vho in da bloomin' blazes is dat?" asked Tobia.
"Looks lik' von of dose hors'less karij," remarked Ed.
Alice jumped to her feet. "I think it's Martin and Jennie. C'mon Palmer, I want you to meet my sister and brother-in-law."
Ardis clung to Palmer like a leech. "Hop on little Buckaroo!"
"Yippee!" Ardis scrambled onto Palmer's back as he rose to follow Alice.
The motorcar rumbled to a stop and Martin shut off the warbling engine. Enthusiasm stirred up like a fire, as the threshing crew gathered around.
"Martin ye got goodt timin' cuz ve yust finish thrashin' da veat," laughed Ed.
"Ye got noses lik' a kupl' of bloodhaunds," chuckled Tobia. "Ye must hav' smel' dat hom' made ic' kream al' da vay fram Williams, Iova." Tobia gave Jennie a big bear hug. "I mis' ye doter, so hape ye cam'!"
"Martin did your horses kick the bucket?" teased Elmer.
"Nei, they're still eatin' me out of house and home!" laughed Martin.
"How fast does that thing go?" asked Jacob.
"About 30 miles per hour," answered Martin.
"Is that a Model T Ford?" asked Eli.
"Ja, it's a 1916 model," informed Martin.
The Ford had a wooden steering wheel, a leather roof, isinglass windows and side running boards. Martin was bombarded with questions from all directions, but he didn't seem to mind.
"How much did that jalopy cost?" asked Elmer.
Martin answered. I gave $200.00 for it. I think I struck a bargin. It's in tiptop shape!"
"Ja, dis model even got sid'lites," said Ed nodding his head in approval.
Martin continued, "If you want a brand spankin' new one, they are $360.00. They threw in the repair kit free. It has a rubber patching kit for the tires, a spare fan belt, transmission bands and even tools to adjust the carburetor. They also gave me that Valvoline can full of gasoline." Martin pointed to the green and white gas can in the back seat.
"Where do you buy the gasoline?" questioned Bjorn.

"Just take your can into the nearest hardware store and they'll refill it."
Walter asked, "Where is the gas tank?"
"It's under the backseat," said Martin lifting up the seat exposing a gas cap between the floorboards. Martin picked up the wooden dipstick that was attached to a string. "You use this stick to tell how much gasoline is still in the tank."
Hans inquired, "What are these pedals for?"
Everyone took turns checking out the 3 diamond-shaped pedals in the shape of a triangle below the driver's seat.
"The left pedal puts it in neutral, it's used as a clutch," explained Martin. "The middle pedal is reverse and the right pedal is your brake."
"I don't think I can fit in there," said Eli shaking his head. "Not enough leg room."
"Oh, they have bigger cars," reported Martin. "You could get an Oldsmobile-Runabout or an Overland Touring car. The price is a little higher though, $850.00. The Roadsters are $600.00 and so are the Ford C-cabs. The cab only seats two or three passengers, but there's lots of leg room and the truck bed would be really handy for hauling cream cans to town."
"You oughta be a motorcar salesman," laughed Jake. "I'm about to get my check book out."
"Ja, I'm thinkin' I gotta have one, too," grinned Olaf.
"Is it hard to learn to drive?" asked Hans.
"Nei, not at all. The greenest plowboy could catch on in no time."
"That's good news for you, Plowboy," teased Palmer grinning at Olaf.
The threshing crew all roared with laughter! And then the enthusiastic chatter continued.
"Have you tried it?" asked Alice looking at her older sister Jennie.
"Nei," Jennie replied, "I'm still trying to get over my riding fears. Martin says if I don't stop all the 'oohs and ahhs', I'll be walking."
"Martin does she squeal like a pig every time you turn a corner?" teased Elmer.
"She does," laughed Martin, "and I told her it's a long walk to town."
"O vel'," chuckled Tobia, "legs vas mad' fer valking."
"Well, I want to learn to drive!" exclaimed Alice.
"Dat dun't surpris' us nun," laughed Ed. "I thout dat vuz comin'. Awww, I reckon ye kin driv' goodt as da men."
"I driv', too!" spouted Ardis who had climbed up another notch onto Palmer's shoulders to get a good look at the motorcar.
Booming laughter came from the crowd!

Jacob spoke up, "Ardis, I think your legs are a wee bit, too short! Son, you better keep eatin' your vegetables."

"Ye yust a lit'l' sapling, but dun't ye vorry nun," soothed Grandpa Ed patting Ardis on the back. "Ye grow up mite lik' oak tree."

Olaf asked, "What's this lever on the steering column?"

"It's your spark."

"How do you start it up?" inquired Walter.

"Looks like Ed is rarin' to go! He's sitting in the driver's seat," laughed Martin. "There are five adjustments you must remember—spark, throttle, emergency brake, choke-wire and key. Ed put the spark lever on 'retard.'"

"Lik' this?" asked Ed.

"That's it!" Pointing at the throttle, Martin instructed, "This gives it gas. Ed put the throttle half way up. The brake handle is the emergency brake and also used for shifting. Ed pinch the handles together and pull it all the way back to the seat." Martin walked back to the front of the car. "See this loop-wire that sticks out on the left side of the radiator."

"Ja, I was wondering what that was for," remarked Elmer.

"It's your choke-wire." Martin grabbed the wire. "Pull it out like this. Now pull up the crank 3 times. This draws more gasoline into the cylinder."

The crowd counted with each revolution. "One...Two...Three..."

"Ed turn the key to the battery position."

"Dun," returned Ed.

Martin grabbed the wooden handle on the crank and pulled up again. The engine sputtered and choked to life.

"Ed put the spark lever back down to the advance position."

"Got it!" hollered Ed.

"Now put the throttle back up!"

"Dun!" returned Ed.

The car moved rhythmically, rocked by the engine.

"Martin, what's her name?" asked Ardis from his perch on Palmer's shoulders.

"Tin Lizzie," laughed Martin. "Who wants to go for a ride in Lizzie?"

"We do!" shouted Alice grabbing Palmer's hand. Her gentle touch sent shivers through him.

"Me too! Me too!" sang Ardis.

Alice and Palmer climbed into the back seat. Palmer put Ardis on his lap.

"Momme, I be rit bak!" shouted Ardis waving at his parents. "Giddy up, Lizzie!"

A roar of laughter came from the crowd!

Elmer added to the laughter by shouting, "Hey, Father! Don't pull back on the steering wheel and shout, 'Whoa!' She'll only go faster."

Martin instructed Ed from the passenger seat. "Put Lizzie in 1st gear. Move the shift handle halfway up and push the clutch, that's the left one, all the way down. Now push the shift handle full forward."

Lizzie rolled forward.

"Now slowly give her some throttle and we're out of here."

Ed swung the Model T Ford into a U-turn and headed down the lane.

"Put the clutch in to slow down and turn," instructed Martin.

Ed turned onto the road and headed toward Thompson.

"Now take your foot off the clutch pedal and Lizzie's in high gear."

The car sped along the country road like a roaring lion leaving a trail of dust. Palmer turned to look at Alice like a flower reaching for the sun. It was a look that penetrated to the depths of Alice heart, a look that said far more than words. They passed by grazing cattle, rustling corn and beautiful wild flowers in the road ditch. Yet they noticed none of those things. Love was breaking out like a bud ready to burst. Alice and Palmer realized they had been bushwhacked by the Love Bug!

Chapter 7   Thompson News Agency

Ed talked about the threshers for days. He claimed he hadn't had that much fun in years. He planned to plant twice as much wheat next year so they would stay longer. When he wasn't talking about threshing, he was talking about driving Martin's Model T Ford.

"Tobia, I dink ve need a motorkar," pleaded Ed.

"I vas skairt ye vas stil' dinkin' 'bout dat," frowned Tobia. "Ye 'no' dose hors's hav' serv'd us vel' fer mange years."

"I 'no', but dose motorkars is da vay of da futur'," pouted Ed. "Ve got to keep up or ve get left in da dust. Tobia yust dink how much tim' it sav' haulin' milk to town. An' ve kud go se' Anna an' da grandatters an' even com' bak in da sam' day."

"Dat's vat trains aur fer!" protested Tobia.

Ignoring Tobia's comment, Ed pressed on. "I dink ve need a Ford C-cab. I sur' kud use dat fer da farm vork. It vud be so hande! I be figurin' an' vith da veat I yust sold, ve got da mone'."

"Edward dat's a lot of mone'! Ye bet'er sleep on it!"

"Dat's da troubl', ven I sleep on it, I dream 'bout motorkars," sighed Ed getting up from the table. "Bet'er git da hors's hi'ched up an' tak' milk to Kremere. Gues' I vil' nam' von of da hors's Lizzie."

Alice spoke up, "Father if you are going to town, I'd like to go. I have Eli's shirt done. I need him to try it on."

"Vith dat heave rain yesterde, I bet he at da Bla'ksmith Shop. Not lik'le dey aur in da field toda'."

Alice had already reasoned that out and she secretly hoped that Palmer might be there, too. Her heart ached to see him again. Their picnic date seemed light-years away. "I need to change my dress. Dolly gave me a good swat with her stinky tail this morning."

"Ye git clean'd up. I git da hors's hi'ched up."

Alice chose her plum rose calico A-line dress with front and back princess seams. It was a simple pattern, but very flattering to her figure. Tobia had added folkloric embroidery, an art she had learned from her mother Enga, so many years ago. The embroidery around the V-notched neckline and the hem of the elbow-length sleeves gave the dress a simple elegance. Alice had used the left-over fabric to make a matching bonnet.

Alice ye luk lov'le," said Tobia proudly. "Ye 'no' dat is mi faveret' dres'. It luks vere becomin' on ye. Ye bet'er tak' y'r shawl. Ye may need it dis mornin'."
Alice reached for her white-knitted shawl. "Thank goodness! That rain finally cooled down the summer sizzle."
Tobia announced, "I hear da jingl' of da harnes', y'r Fader is comin'."
Ed pulled up with the horses and wagon. Queen was a white mare with a splash of gray on her forehead. Her mane and tail were dark gray also. Her partner a chestnut mare was named Nelly. She had a black mane and black socks. The two were a well-matched driving team. The old, gentle mares had been part of the family as long as Alice could remember.
"Giddap dere gals!" Ed shook the reins to urge the horses forward.
The heavy, soaking rain yesterday gave the air a new freshness and the smell of damp earth was everywhere.
Alice looked up at the clear, blue sky. The same color blue as Palmer's captivating eyes. She wondered at the strange feelings within her lovesick heart. He was so good-natured. Ardis had attached himself to Palmer like a cocklebur. What was there not to like? His calm, low voice was so kind and reassuring. A voice that was as impressive as his looks. His gentle manner had unlocked Alice's heart. He would make a good husband and father. Alice had basked in the thought of becoming Palmer's wife for days. A thought she didn't want to erase.
Ed broke into her thoughts, "Alice lukee at dat corn. I dink it shot up a foot last nite fram dat goodt rain."

~~~~~~

Rainy days were always busy at John Helgren's Blacksmith Shop. Gunvor Torgeson had brought in a broken part for his manure spreader.
"Kin yah, mak' a nu von?" he asked John.
"Sure, I don't think it will be a problem," answered John.
"Spreder brok' down vith a full load on thar. I had to pitch it all off by hand." Palmer and Eli burst out laughing.
"Next tim' it happen, I com' git ye two strong, young fellows. Den ye wun't be laughin' so hardt!" exclaimed Gunvor.
"Yup!" grinned Eli. "No time for laughin'. Back to the grindstone."
"Hey, vhat's dis I hear 'bout ye carryin' a cream can?" asked Gunvor.
"Oh, it was nothing," said Eli modestly.

"Well, I was impressed," returned John. "Your great feat of strength has been the talk of the town."

"It was a fool thing to do," admitted Eli. "Only an idiot would bet with Oscar Vage!"

"I can take it out of his wages," offered Palmer.

"Nei, he needs it to feed all those children of his," said Eli with concern.

"How many children does he have?" asked John.

Palmer answered, "Eight and when he told me he had another one on the way, he was smiling like a cat who just ate the canary."

"Does he 'no' vhat causes dat?" questioned Gunvor.

"It's hard to say," said Eli. "Sometimes Oscar ain't got the sense of a hop-toad."

"Does he farm?" inquired Gunvor.

Palmer nodded, "He inherited forty acres from his father. He farms it with mules or maybe I should say his wife and children do."

"Vhat's he rais' fer crops?" asked Gunvor.

John answered, "It sounds like he mostly raises young 'uns."

"I 'spect dat so," said Gunvor as he roared with laughter.

Eli and Palmer continued assembling the new wagon that Henry Larson had ordered.

Palmer tried to concentrate on the task at hand, but he was starting to entertain serious thoughts about Alice. In fact, it was impossible to get her out of his mind. Palmer loved the way her face sparkled with laughter. Her big, brown eyes spoke volumes without words. Her voice was sweet and musical. It was all etched in his memory. An undeniable seed of admiration was growing deep inside. It had sprouted and flourished within Palmer's heart. He was resolved to win Alice for his bride or perish in the attempt.

Eli broke into Palmer's thoughts. "You've been smilin' like a goofy kid, Palmer. A girl like Alice can do that to a fellow. How many days until the picnic?"

"Too many," sighed Palmer and the thought left a lingering ache.

"You could call her," suggested Eli.

"That would really get those old biddies going! They use that telephone like a grapevine to spread their venomous slander," grimaced Palmer.

"Ja, news travels like a speeding bullet around here," agreed Eli. "One of these days their hot gossip is goin' to burn up the lines!"

Eli lifted the rear end of the wagon and Palmer put a wooden wheel on Henry's wagon.

~~~~~~

Soon Ed and Alice could see the buildings huddled together on the Main Street of Thompson. They passed the Willow Creek Sawmill and Lumberyard, next came the Thompson Ice House. In front of the Blacksmith Shop was a black gelding. *Could that be Palmer's horse*? Hope surged through Alice.

"I drop ye off an' ye kin tak' car' of y'r bizness while I tak' milk to da kremere," suggested Ed.

"Good that will save time."

Ed pulled up in front of Erickson's General Store. **"Whoa, gals!"** ordered Ed as he pulled back on the reins.

Alice hurried into the store. "Good morning, Mr. Erickson!"

"Alice you sure do look nice today. Bet you made that dress."

"I did indeed," giggled Alice. "But Mother added the folkloric embroidery."

"If Tobia wants another job, I'm sure we can keep her very busy," laughed Elias.

"Thank you, but she already has too many irons in the fire and they're all red hot."

"Emma come and see this dress Miss Alice made," hollered Elias to his wife who was stocking shelves at the back of the store.

"Oh, Alice, that's so beautiful! You are a very talented young lady," complimented Emma.

"Thank you! You are both so kind."

"Now what are you needin' today?" asked Elias.

"Some fabric and more sewing supplies."

"Oh, we've got a deal for you," offered Emma. "Come this way dear."

Just then the doorbell jangled and Gyda Yawnson waltzed into the store. She had a excellent reputation as Thompson's News Agency. Gyda lived on the telephone and spread incurable gossip like a blazing prairie fire. Her tongue which never stopped moving could out wag any dog's tail. And if that wasn't enough, she was a shameless flirt. Gyda strutted right passed Alice and Emma as if they were invisible.

"Yoo-hoo! Why Elias, you sure do look charming today. You know, there oughta be a law against men as handsome as you," giggled Gyda leaning across the counter to expose her big bosom which she had drawn up to giddy heights. Her waist was pinched into a dress three sizes too small and the pleated skirt of her dress flared out over her big fanny.

"What can I help you with today?" asked Elias.

"Oh, my dear if you only knew all the things you could help me with, but first things first. I know you hear lots of interesting facts every day, so I thought you might want to share the latest news in town with me. You know the telephone is a great invention. I shall be grateful to Alexander Graham Bell eternally, but I like to get my news first hand, right from the horse's mouth. It's absolutely the best way, of course." Gyda was regular as clockwork, stopping daily to try to glean some new tidbits to spice up her humdrum life.

Emma spouted, "Why not check at the newspaper office?"

"Oh, land sakes!" exclaimed Gyda. "I didn't know you were here Emma!"

"Obviously," remarked Emma under her breath. "I only live here."

"Oh, Alice, don't you look lovely today? I know some eligible bachelors who are still unattached!"

I'm sure you know them all, thought Alice.

"I'm not talking about some no-account cowhands. I'm talking about good stock, real men if you get my drift. There's only a few out there. No time to waste, my dear. You gotta get one while the gettin's good. Strike when the irons hot! Always remember the two P's. If he's got a pulse and a paycheck, go for it! I've got excellent taste when it comes to men. I won't steer you in the wrong direction."

Gyda babbled on, "I just heard a rumor about Eli Olafsen. Of course, it's just a rumor you know. I personally don't really believe it! I think it's just a bit of rubbish just to amuse the single girls like you Alice. But I must admit that man has got some brawny muscles and the looks to boot. A mighty good catch if I say so myself, but I'm willing to share. Eli works at the Blacksmith Shop. I could introduce you if you'd like."

"No need," said Alice. "I've already met Eli."

"Oh, really! My goodness is there something new I should know about?" ventured Gyda.

Emma with a look of disgust on her face interrupted, "If there was something new, I'm sure you'd be the first to know."

Ignoring Emma's remark, Gyda jabbered on, "I was just wondering if there are any wedding plans in the near future? You know I'm very good at that sort of thing!"

Of course, she's good at wedding plans, thought Emma. *She's been married three times or is it four?*

"No," Alice replied. "Now if you will excuse me, I'd like to look at the fabric."

"We have lots of new bolts of fabric," announced Emma leading the way. And a special deal this month, too. See the dress our mannequin is wearing?"

Alice smiled, "Yes, I love it!"

"Well the pattern is free when you buy five or more yards of fabric. And for every ten yards of fabric you buy, you get a yard free."

Alice was excited. With the money from Eli's threshing check, she would be buying a lot of fabric and could take advantage of this good deal.

Elias was waiting on a customer, so Gyda had strolled to the fabric section. She had been eavesdropping, a daily occurrence for Gyda.

"These run-of-the-mill folks here in Thompson don't have the money for that deal!" scowled Gyda. "That's a cute dress on the mannequin. I'd try it on, but the neckline is too high for me."

Emma thought *that dress is ten sizes too small for you!*

Alice stared wide-eyed at the large selection of fabric. There were so many choices; paisley, floral, gingham and sprigged prints, calicos in every color, black satine, poplin, unbleached cotton, fine linen, denim, flannels and corduroy.

"I sure do like that sun hat," cackled Gyda pointing at the wide-brimmed straw hat on the mannequin. The hat was trimmed with pink piping around the edge and had a matching bow. Gyda grabbed the hat and checked the price tag. "Oo-oo! I think I've struck a bargain! It's only two dollars," she squealed. Gyda pressed the hat on top of her heaped up hairdo. "Well I sure hope there's a mirror in this country bumpkin store," smirked Gyda.

Emma pointed towards the hat boxes. "It's over there by the hats and hair ribbons."

Alice handed Emma a bolt of blue and white pin-striped fabric, remembering Eli's favorite color.

"We have that same print in navy," stated Emma.

"I like it," said Alice pulling it off the shelf. Alice added another bolt of sky blue cotton to the stack in Emma's arms.

That will match Eli's merry blue eyes, thought Alice. "I need five yards of the striped and two and a half of the blue."

"I'll be right back," said Emma leaving with her load.

"Egads! Alice what are you going to do with all that fabric?" queried Gyda.

Alice sensed a storm approaching. She wished Gyda would get lost, but she was still rooted there with hands on her hips, waiting for an explanation.

Slim chance of her leaving in the near future, thought Alice. "I have a sewing job," said Alice cautiously.

"Oh, I didn't know you were a seamstress."

Alice pulled a bolt of sandy-brown cotton, one of steel-gray and a third one of burgundy plaid.

"Alice are you sewing for the whole township?" blurted Gyda.

"Just a friend," said Alice softly.

"Well who's the friend?" inquired Gyda as she hovered beside Alice.

Alice thought, *I'm going to gag you with a piece of fabric if you persist in antagonizing me!*

"Well, I'm waiting, speak up girl!" screeched Gyda. "Who's the friend?"

Alice saw Emma returning and called out, "Emma do you think this lavender wildflower print would work with the new pattern?"

"That's my favorite print," announced Emma. "I want to see the dress when you're done."

Alice handed the bolts of fabric to Emma. "I'll need two yards of each."

"I'll get it cut off," returned Emma as she headed for the counter.

Alice quickly gathered up thread, white piping for trim and buttons. She headed for the cash register with Gyda on her heels.

Alice that's a lot of buttons. Are you sewing shirts?" questioned Gyda.

"Yes," answered Alice.

"Well how many times do I have to ask you? Who are the shirts for?"

"They're for Eli."

"Oh, my, my! I guess you do know Eli Olafsen. So you have been checking out those big, brawny muscles, haven't you? Measuring and measuring and measuring!"

Elias interrupted, "Gyda if you're not going to buy that hat, please put it back."

Gyda ignored Elias for the very first time in history and droned on, "Oh, my dear, you are young and foolish! Let me give you some good advice. You need to secure a husband before you go to all this trouble. All this hard work leaves little time for pleasantries."

Alice was saved when Ed walked in. "Almost ready Father."

"Your lavender print is free and so is the pattern," said Emma adding them to the box.

"Thank you!" Alice handed the money to Emma.

"Egads! Did you rob the bank?" cried Gyda. "Or have you been digging in Eli's pockets?"

Ignoring Gyda, Alice said, "Thank you, Emma! You have been most helpful."

"Thank you, Alice! And don't forget to stop by and show off your new dress."

"I will," promised Alice.

Ed grabbed the box, "Mange Takk!"

"Velkommen," returned Elias who only knew a few Norwegian words. "We appreciate your business!"

Ed put the box in the back of the wagon. Their next stop was the Blacksmith Shop. Gyda threw the hat on the counter. She wanted to see where the Hoverstens were going. "Oo—oo! I'll be right back! I daresay, I've got a strong hunch there's something big goin' on around here!" She raced outside letting the door slam behind her.

"Her Royal Highness can talk the hind legs off a mule," laughed Elias.

"I'm not laughing," said Emma. "That floozy treats people like they're pond scum! I hope she doesn't start trouble for Alice."

Gyda hustled down the wooden boardwalk and ran smack into her telephone accomplice, Bertina Fardal.

"Where in the thunder have you been?" spurted Bertina breathlessly. "I've been ringin' your telephone right off the wall."

"Oo—oo!" Gyda squawked. "I'm onto something really Big! No proof yet, but I'm about to unravel the whole skein of yarn if you know what I mean. C'mon we've got to get closer so we can investigate."

The women hurried along huffing and puffing.

"Look! Bertina they just went into the Blacksmith Shop. That's exactly what I thought would happen."

"Maybe, we can peek in the window," exploded Bertina with a rush of excitement. "Hurry!"

"Oh, I wish I hadn't worn these high heel shoes," whined Gyda.

~~~~~~

"Haloo neighbor," said Ed shaking Gunvor's hand.

"How ye been? Dis must be Alice? She's all grown up an' purte as a wildflower. Ed it's time to lock her in da attic!" Gunvor bellowed with laughter.

Alice felt her cheeks blush crimson red.

Palmer couldn't keep his eyes off Alice. He felt a strange sensation taking place, a rush of excitement that he'd never known before. He almost tripped over the wagon tongue, but reached out with his hand and steadied himself against the wagon box. He finally found his voice. "Father this is Ed Hoversten and his daughter, Alice."

John nodded, "I've met Ed before, but I didn't know he had such a beautiful daughter."

Alice felt her cheeks burning again. *I must look like a tomato head by now.* She managed to get out a, "thank you!"

Eli was trimming the hooves of a big Belgian draft horse. He noticed the shirt hanging over Alice's arm. "Alice, do you need me to try on that shirt?"

Ed spoke up. "Finish y'r job first. Ve aur in no hure."

"On the last hoof," reported Eli.

Gunvor interrupted, "Ed, I sur' am sorre mi bull yump da fenc'. He leaps fenc's lik' a deer. He's got a mind of his own. Kin't keep heem in."

"Gues' he dinks da grass is greener on da ot'er sid' of da fenc'," laughed Ed. "No harm dun, he vas in vith da kows. I keep da youn' heifers in pastur' north of haus'."

"Did ye git ane heifer calves out of heem?"

"Ja, I sur' did. Even git a set of twins. He a goodt bul'," bragged Ed.

Gyda and Bertina finally reached the Blacksmith Shop. When they recovered from their panting, they peeked into the side window.

"Miss Alice, I smell pretty bad. Do you want me to step outside and clean up a bit?" asked Eli wiping his hands on his torn trousers.

Alice handed him the shirt. "Nei, your fine, Eli."

"You bet he's fine," whispered Gyda.

Eli stepped behind the big draft horse and peeled off his old, sweaty shirt.

"Oo—oo! O—oo! That man's got more muscle than the horse," gasped Gyda.

"Shhhh," whispered Bertina. "They might hear you."

Eli stepped out with his new blue shirt on, grinning ear to ear. "It fits like a glove!" He gave Alice his well-done nod. "How did you get it done so fast?"

Ed answered, "Tobia's rit, Alice sews lik' a hummingbird."

"Eli, I need to get one more measurement for the long-sleeved shirts with your elbow bent. I forgot that one," explained Alice.

"Of course, she did," murmured Gyda. "She's one smart girl."

"Hush," warned Bertina pressing a finger to her pursed lips.

Ed dug in his pocket and retrieved the paper measuring tape handing it to Alice.

"Good idea," smiled Eli. "I can always use more elbow room!" Eli flapped his elbows like chicken wings and laughter erupted from the men.

"Oh, that girl does love to measure," blurted Gyda. "Maybe I'll take up sewing."

Bertina advised, "You better quiet down Gyda. They'll hear us. What if we get caught?"

"Oh, we'll just tell Eli we need our buggy brakes checked," smirked Gyda.

"Should I set you up on this big Belgian, so you can reach?" asked Eli as a big grin split his face.

Palmer came to Alice's rescue. "I'll hold the top half for you."

Gyda who is that tall, good-lookin' blonde?" whispered Bertina.

Gyda's eyes gleamed with excitement. "I'm not sure. Oh, he is handsome, isn't he? How I hope he's single. I guess I'll have to get a job at the Blacksmith Shop."

"Well, I can't believe it," whispered Bertina. "I thought you knew all the men around here."

"I guess one got away," pouted Gyda. "Trust me; I'm working on a plan to fix that right away."

Looking at Eli's torn trousers, Alice said, "Eli there's a lot of money left. Could you use some new pants?"

"How'd you guess?" laughed Eli. "I'll bring you an old pair and you can use them for a pattern."

"That would be a big help," replied Alice.

"Wow, that girl is good," whispered Bertina.

"Yes," agreed Gyda. "She lined up another date and Eli didn't even catch on. I bet there will be more measuring going on."

"Ve best be movin' along," said Ed. "Gunvor if ye need help vith dat spreder, I be glad to giv' helpin' hand."

"Mange Takk! But dink I kin fix it dis tim'," chuckled Gunvor.

The men followed the Hoverstens to the wagon.

"Eli, Gyda knows I'm sewing shirts for you. I hope it doesn't cause you any grief."

"That woman is a drain on my time!" exclaimed Eli. "Hangs around here like she's trying to grow roots. I told John; maybe we could use her for a fly trap. She oughta be able to catch a full mouth of flies with that big gapin' hole in her face." Everyone roared with laughter as Gyda and Bertina peeked around the corner hoping to collect a juicy story for their Thompson News Agency.

"Gyda look," whispered Bertina, "here comes Emma down the boardwalk. She saw us spying."

"I'll fix that! Follow me," commanded Gyda. "Yoo-hoo! Gentlemen, oh and Alice, it's nice to see you again. This is my friend Bertina Fardal. We're out for our morning stroll. It is such a lovely day, don't you think? We couldn't stay at home in that stuffy old house not one minute longer. Of course, we were stuck inside all day yesterday, because of that dreadful rain storm and we needed to get out and soak up some sunshine. Oh, I don't think I've met you." Gyda stopped babbling

long enough to extend her hand to Palmer. "I'm Gyda Yawnson and who might you be?"
Palmer graciously extended his hand. "I'm Palmer Helgren, John's oldest son."
"Oh, I'm so thrilled to meet you. Tell me all about yourself. Are you single?"
Just then Emma interrupted, "Mr. Hoversten, Tobia just called. Edna has gone into labor. Can you swing by their house and pick up Ardis?"
"Tel' her ve're on aur vay. Mange Takk, Emma!" Ed shook the reins, **"Giddap dere gals!!!** I sure could use a motorkar rit now."
Gyda and Bertina grinned ear to ear. Top-notch news right from the horse's mouth for their Thompson News Agency.

Chapter 8   Itty Bitty Baby

Ed let Queen and Nelly plod along at their own slow pace. Ardis sat on Ed's lap helping hold the reins. Alice's mind was busy designing her new dress. *I like the full sweep skirt, but that would take a lot of fabric. There's a scrap of lavender fabric in my stash pile. I could make the bodice and sleeve cuffs out of that. Then I could use the wildflower print for the sleeves and skirt.*
Ed's voice broke into her thoughts, **"Whoa dere gals!"**
Ardis chimed in, "Whoa Nelly! Whoa Queen!"
Alice hurried into the house with her box of fabric while Ed and Ardis headed for the barn to take care of the horses.
Tobia was in the kitchen putting butter-cream icing on her chocolate cake. "How is Edna doin'?"
"Edna's fine," giggled Alice. "It's Jacob we're worried about."
"Is Rachel dere?" asked Tobia.
"Ja Mother, no need to worry. She's got everything under control. Well except for Jacob that is."
"I sur' hope Edna hav' gerl dis tim'. I yust finish knittin' pink bon'et an' bo'ties."
"I sure hope so, too. The baby quilt I made has lots of pink in it. Mother look at this pattern. I got it free and the fabric, too."
"I lov' dat flauer print," nodded Tobia, but dat paturn luk too hardt."
"The scalloped neck and hemline do look difficult," agreed Alice, "but I love a challenge. I want to wear this new dress to the picnic."
"Land sakes, Doter! Ye bet'er grow vings an' fly den."
Alice was cutting out her dress when she heard the telephone ring. **Ring!! Ring!! R-i-n-g**...
"Two short rings an' von long, dat's aur numbur. I git it, Alice!" Soon Tobia appeared in the doorway. "Edna hav' babe gerl. Run down to da barn an' tel' Fader to hi'ch up hors's ag'in."
Alice found Ardis playing with the new kittens, while Ed was mucking out Queen's stall.
"Ardis your new sister is here!" exclaimed Alice with excitement.
Ardis clapped his little hands, "I a big broder!"
"Yes!" Alice grabbed Ardis into her arms and swung him around. "Mother wants you to hitch up the horses again."
"Dis is vhy ve need a motorkar," barked Ed.

Jacob met them at the door with a little bundle in his arms.
Ardis bolted into the house and announced, "I big broder now!"
"Son you sure are. Meet your new sister, Norrene."
"Can she play with me?" asked Ardis.
"Nei, she's too little. She can't walk yet," answered Jacob.
"I can learn her to walk," said Ardis beaming with pride.
"Not just yet, son," laughed Jacob. "What's in that basket Mother? I'm starving!"
"Ye always starvin'!" declared Tobia. "Ye nurs' lik' a pig vhen ye vas born an' ye stil' eat lik' von. How ye stay so thin?"
"It's called hard work Mother. If you work like a horse you have to eat like one, too."
Ed came to Jacob's defense, "Tobia ye dun't muzzl' da ox when it thrashin'."
"I'll trad' ye chakolet cak' fer dat lit'l babe," begged Tobia.
Jacob handed over his new treasure and Tobia headed for the rocking chair.
"Don't eat the basket Jacob," giggled Alice.
Jacob returned, "Never little sister, I want you womenfolk to keep refilling it."
Tobia rocked her new granddaughter and sang the Pat-a-cake song in Norwegian.
"Dat's mi song," said Ardis.
"I yusto sing it to ye vhen ye vas an itty bitty babe."
Ardis asked, "I vas itty bitty lik' dat?"
"Ye sur' vas," chuckled Ed. "Held y'r lit'l head in da palm of mi big hand."
"Yup! And now I a big broder," said Ardis.
"It's my turn," begged Ed reaching for the new baby.
Tobia reluctantly handed over the itty bitty baby.
"Yust luk at dis lit'l button nos'," said Ed.
"She's so beautiful," crooned Alice.
"Yust vhat ve ordered," bragged Ed.
Ardis gently stroked Norrene's little hand, "She got itty bitty fingers, too." And then he raced over to Jacob with his mouth wide open like a little birdie.
"You little vulture," said Jacob forking in a bite of cake.
"He's a lit'l birdie an' ye aur da vultur'," chuckled Tobia.
Ed handed Norrene to Alice and looked out the window. "Elmer an' Josie aur here."
"Jacob it looks like you'll have to share your cake with another big vulture," giggled Alice.

"We came to see the new baby," said Elmer barging through the front door. "Oh, she is a beauty! You did good big brother." As always, Elmer gave Jacob a hearty slap on the back.

"I think Edna should get a little credit, don't you think?" asked Josie.

"Ja, I must confess, she helped out a little bit," laughed Jacob. "I just read a quote from Mark Twain in the newspaper this morning. It said: 'What would men be without women? Scarce, sir...Mighty scarce.'"

"I should say so!" exclaimed Edna coming out of the bedroom.

"I tried to keep her in bed," explained Rachel, "but our new mother wants to enjoy the pleasure of your company."

"Put her in da rocker," advised Tobia getting up.

"Oh, don't fuss over me," insisted Edna. "Sweet Rachel has been waiting on me head to toe."

"This is Rachel Allison, our midwife," announced Jacob. "Rachel this is my parents, Tobia and Edward, my sister Alice, my brother Elmer and his wife Josie."

"It's so nice to meet you," said Rachel.

"And you, too!" chimed the Hoverstens.

"Mange takk fer takin' ker' of aur Edna an' babe Norrene," replied Tobia.

Elmer stood up. "I have an announcement to make. My beautiful wife Josephine is with child."

When the round of applause died down, Jacob extended his right hand to Elmer. "Congratulations, little brother!" He shook Elmer's hand fiercely and with his left hand he gave Elmer a hearty slap on the back. "Why you ol' rascal. You better get some sleep now. When that baby gets here you'll be mos' dead for sleep. Your life will be topsy-turvy."

Ardis mimicked his father. "Topsy-turvy, topsy-turvy," he sang as he spun in circles in the center of the living room.

"Jes' luk at heem!" chuckled Tobia. "Ye goin' to git dizze."

"Topsy-turvy dizzy," sang Ardis spinning.

"Never a dull moment with Ardis around," giggled Alice.

"Listen, dat saunds lik' a motorkar comin'," said Ed looking out the window. "It is a motorkar!"

"Vho in da blumin' blaz's is dat?" asked Tobia.

Ardis jumped up and down clapping his hands, "Lizzie's comin'!"

"Jumpin' Jehoshaphat!" cried Jacob. "If they keep comin' at this pace, we'll have to knock out a wall for more space. Let them in, I'll grab some more chairs from the dining room."

Ed opened the screen door. "Wel' haloo Eli! C'mon in!"

Eli entered the house with two big baskets of food. Rachel couldn't stop staring. This tall man's broad shoulders filled the doorway. He was breathtakingly handsome with his wind-blown blonde hair and merry blue eyes. "Mother made ham and beans and Johnnie cake for ya'll."

"How kind! Please thank Olivia for us," insisted Edna.

"I stopped at Erickson's Store to get a jug of maple syrup for the cornbread and I found this music box for the baby." Eli handed it to Edna. "It plays the 'Mocking Bird' lullaby."

Rachel thought Eli's calm, soothing voice sounded like a lullaby.

"Oh Eli, Ardis loves that song and I know Norrene will, too. Thank you!"

Ardis twirling in circles started singing, *"Hush littl' baby don't say a word, Mama's goin' buy you a mocking bird..."*

Jacob set a chair for Eli next to Rachel. "Rachel this is Eli Olafsen."

Eli reached down and extended his big hand giving Rachel a hearty handshake. "Nice to meetcha!"

Jacob continued, "and this is Rachel Allison."

"It's nice to meet you, too, Eli."

Eli was thunderstruck by Rachel's stunning beauty! Her voice was soft and gentle. The kind of voice that sings babies to sleep. Her features were lovely, delicate, and feminine. Long lashes framed her beautiful soft amber eyes. Her cheeks had a rosy glow. Her sparkling smile revealed straight white teeth. Her thick mahogany curls cascaded about her shoulders. Eli slowly released her hand, praying he hadn't crushed it. He swallowed a big gulp of spit and sat down next to her. "Are you Dr. Allison's daughter?"

"Yes, I'm the oldest," replied Rachel.

"I met your father at John's Blacksmith Shop and your sister Mary when we were threshing for the Hoverstens."

"Looks like you've met us all except for Mary's twin, Malenda. So you are the man who carried the cream can to the well and back. Now that I've met you, I believe every word of the tale."

"Oh, it was nothing! It was a fool thing to do. I've learned my lesson. I'll never bet again."

Elmer interrupted, "What do you mean, it was nothing? It was awesome!"

"Ja, ve not hav' dat much fun in a long tim'," offered Ed.

Jacob nodded, "I think Oscar's the one that learned a good lesson. I'll never forget the expression on Oscar's face when you threatened to stick his head in a cowpie. He looked like he'd swallowed a big old horsefly."

When the laughter quieted down Ed asked, "Is dat y'r motorkar Eli?"

"Ja, I bought it from Mr. Ellwood. He decided to get a new one."

Jacob asked, "What kind of car is that?"

'It's an Oldsmobile Runabout. It's got lots of room. I needed the extra space for my long legs."

"It sur' is a goodt lukin' motorkar!" exclaimed Ed, staring at it through the screen door. "It's a real humdinger!"

"How much did you have to give for it?" queried Elmer.

"I gave $400.00 for it. It's only 2 years old and the new ones are $850.00."

"That's a steal!" blurted Jacob. "I wish I could find one like that."

Alice asked, "Eli would you like to hold the baby?"

"I don't think I know how Alice. I might break her. She looks like a little china doll."

"There's nothing to it," said Alice as she placed the itty bitty baby in the crook of Eli's elbow.

"She's the prettiest little thing I ever did see. Perfect little rosebud mouth," said Eli tenderly.

Ardis touched Norrene's little hand, "she's itty bitty babe."

"That she is. I'm sure I was never itty bitty," smiled Eli.

Ardis had no idea why the adults were laughing, but he clapped his hands anyway.

"Rachel how long have you been a midwife?" asked Josie.

"Since I was seven years old," laughed Rachel.

"Really, what happened?" asked Edna.

"I started going with Mother when I was about five. My job was to run after things and comfort the birthing mothers. I was about seven when Mother ran into serious trouble. We had been up all night and still no baby. The mother was exhausted and had given up. My mother was exhausted also. She had tried and tried to turn the baby to no avail. In desperation, she looked at my small hands and told me to follow her instructions exactly. The baby flipped and the little fellow slipped right into my arms. From that day on, Mother had me turn all the breech babies."

Edna asked, "Where did you get the idea to use a birth chair?"

"It's in the Bible."

"It is," queried Edna. "Jacob bring us the Bible."

Rachel opened the Bible to Exodus, Chapter 1 and explained. "The Israelites were slaves in Egypt, but 'they multiplied and grew exceedingly strong'. This frightened the new Pharaoh so he made this command to the midwives. Starting with verse 15 it says: 'Then the king of Egypt said to the Hebrew midwives, one of whom was named Shiphrah and the other Puah, when you serve as midwife to the Hebrew women and see them upon the birthstool, if it is a son, you shall kill him; but if it is a daughter, she shall live.' These two courageous midwives feared the true God and they did not obey Pharaoh."

"Rachel, I'm so glad you are a Bible reader," said Edna.

"Mother always said the best place to look for good advice is in the Bible. And my new mothers claim the birth-chair is easier for them and no stitches."

"Amen to that!" exclaimed Edna. "Rachel I can't praise you enough. You are a very gifted midwife."

"Thank you! You are so kind. I love my job. I never get tired of seeing the miracle of life."

Eli added, "I'll never get tire of holding this itty bitty baby, but she's starting to squirm. Do you think she's getting hungry?"

Rachel looked at her wristwatch. "It's been almost 4 hours since she nursed. Jacob this one might be a sleeper."

"Hallujah!" cried Jacob.

"Vhat ye whinin' 'bout? Y'r vife gits up to nurs' babe," spouted Tobia.

"I get itty bitty babe a cookie," offered Ardis.

"No cookie, the jar's empty and she doesn't eat cookies," explained Jacob.

"What does she eat?" asked Ardis.

Jacob answered, "she drinks mommy's milk."

"She grow up to eat kukes soon enof," chuckled Ed.

Tobia spouted, "I s'pose she be a kuke thief lik' her fader."

"I brought a basket of cookies. I'll refill your cookie jar Jacob," offered Josie.

"Josie, did I ever tell you what a wonderful sister-in-law you are?" smiled Jacob.

"R-i-n-g, r-i-n-g, ring!! "2 long, 1 short- that's our number," said Jacob jumping up to get the telephone.

Eli asked, "Have you held the baby Josie?"

Josie sprang to her feet. "I'd love to hold that itty bitty baby."

Jacob returned with the telephone message. "Rachel that was Henry Larson. He sounded pretty shook. Eva's gone into labor and not making any progress. She claims this time is different from her other births. They need you to come quickly! I'll saddle your horse."

"Thank you, I'll grab my black bag, it's in the bedroom."
Eli jumped up rising to his impressive height. "Why not take my car? We'll be there in half the time." Without waiting for an answer he started toward the door. "I'll get it started."
Rachel stepped out the front door. Eli thought she looked wildly beautiful! She had a tall, slender profile. The sunlight highlighted her bronzed skin and glowing mahogany hair. *She is gorgeous*! "What would she want with a big oaf like me?" Eli asked himself.
They sped along at top speed in Eli's Oldsmobile Runabout.
Rachel spoke first "Eli I hate to ask this of you, but I may need your help. I'm afraid Eva's baby is breech."
"My Lady, I am at your beck and call. I shall do whatever you ask."
"Thank you, Kind Sir. Eli you are a knight in shining armor rescuing maidens in distress with your Oldsmobile Runabout."
Laughter diffused some of the tension and worry associated with the challenging situation that lie ahead.
"'A joyful heart is good medicine...'" quoted Eli.
"Proverbs 17:22, Eli is a Bible reader. That's one of my favorite scriptures."
With a more serious tone Rachel continued, "I'm upset with Henry. I asked him to make a birth-chair last year when Samuel was born."
"Let me guess. Henry said, 'I'll get around to it later.'"
"That's exactly what he said," agreed Rachel.
"Ja, that's what he always says. The problem is later never comes."
"Well, we really need one now. If you can find a stump about a foot tall and hollow it out cutting away about one-third from the front."
"I'll check the woodpile first thing," stated Eli.
"Thanks Eli! I just hope we have enough time. Otherwise we'll have to come up with another plan."

~~~~~~

On the way home Queen and Nelly plodded along at their own slow pace pulling the rattling buggy.
Tobia piped up, "Edward, don't ye dink it's 'bout tim' to buy a motorkar? Vhat in da blumin' blazes aur ye vaitin' fer?"
Ed was speechless!

Chapter 9 Sadie

Rachel hollered, "Father I'm going out to make my rounds. I need to check in on all my new mothers and babies!"

Doctor Allison stepped out of his office. "These womenfolk around here sure do keep you busy."

Rachel countered, "That's the fault of the men!"

"I reckon so," laughed Doc.

Rachel mounted her horse and headed west. She had Sadie Vage on her mind. Sadie's life was one of mere existence. Rachel was Sadie's only friend and only link to the outside world. Past memories flooded Rachel's mind. Rachel was eight years old when Sadie gave birth to her first child. It was then that Sadie revealed her tragic lot in life to Rachel and her mother. Sadie's father, in a drunken rage, had traded Sadie for one of Oscar's mules. There was something wrong with this story. Rachel had tried to figure it out for years. What kind of father trades his child for a mule? Gives her to a man at least 20 years older than her. Would it always remain an unsolved mystery? Rachel's mother had examined Sadie's head and found a terrible scar, but Sadie couldn't remember hitting her head. Sadie said she had been very sick with severe headaches and depression. She was frightened because she had lost most of her memory. She couldn't remember her family, where she grew up, or even how she got here. She was grateful that she could remember songs and Bible verses she had learned as a child. It helped her deal with her depression. Rachel's mother had delivered Sarah, Ruth, David and Sadie's twin girls, Leah and Lydia. After Caroline's death, Rachel, at the age of sixteen, became the mid-wife for King township. Rachel delivered Sadie's sixth child, her name-sake, a little girl named Rachel. The last two were identical twin boys, Joel and Jonathan. Rachel crossed the plank bridge over Willow Creek. Just around the bend was Palmer Helgren's farm to the north. The next lane to the south was the Vage farm.

~~~~~~

Sadie leaned forward on her milk stool and pressed her forehead against the warm flank of Buttercup. She sang, *"Shoo-fly don't bother me..."* in her soft soothing sing-song voice. Buttercup seemed to swish her tail to the tune as frothy warm milk filled up Sadie's wooden bucket.

Her eight year old son, David appeared at the barn door. "Mama, Miss Rachel is here."

"I'll be right there. David, please turn Buttercup out to pasture." Sadie crossed the yard with her heavy pail sending chickens cackling and fluttering away. Sadie pulled a threadbare dish towel off the clothes line, covered her bucket and lowered it down in the well. It was the only way she could cool her milk during the summer.

The children were all gathered around Rachel. Oscar did not permit Sadie or the children to leave the farm. So a visitor to their home was a special day indeed. Sarah the twelve year old carried Jonathan on her hip. Ruth just two years younger packed around the other twin, Joel. Leah and Lydia, the six year old twins were trying to lug, Tabby, the barn cat around. Rachel held her name-sake, a little blue-eyed blossom in her arms.

Sadie ran to Rachel and wrapped her petite, thin arms around her. Tears streamed down her face, "I have missed you so much!" Sadie wore a weariness that attested to her extreme exhaustion. "We have a surprise for you," announced Sadie, drying her tears on her faded apron.

"I've missed you, too," consoled Rachel with a voice full of worried concern.

Sandy-headed David came across the yard with a rag tied around his foot limping like a bird with a broken wing.

"David what happened to your foot?" asked Rachel with compassion.

"We took bath in the creek last nite," explained David. "A sharp stone cut me."

"We better take a look at that," suggested Rachel pulling her black bag out of the saddlebag.

Sadie sat David down on a tree stump and went to the well for some clean water. Rachel removed the rag-bandage to take a look. "The good news is that it doesn't need stitches, but we need to keep this wound clean. Do you have shoes David?"

"Nei," the young lad shook his head.

"How about a sock?" queried Rachel.

"I'll get one," offered Sarah dragging the sagging screen door open with its huge, gaping-zigzag-hole.

Rachel cleaned and bandaged the wound and then covered it with the old worn sock. "Sadie, I'll leave some Epsom salts so you can soak David's foot. We don't want this wound to get infected."

"Thank you, Miss Rachel!" spouted David.

"You are so welcome," said Rachel tenderly giving David a kiss on the forehead.

David's cheeks blushed red and Sadie explained, "He thinks he's too old for kisses."

Rachel returned, "Kisses are good medicine. I recommend them daily."

"I hungre," cried Leah.

"Me too," agreed little Rachel.

"Rachel, I have to feed the children and then we'll show you our surprise," promised Sadie.

"I'll help you," offered Rachel.

Years and weather had taken a toll on the old, log cabin, Sadie called home. The wooden shingles were growing a bumper crop of moss. The weight of the roof had punished the sagging porch, propped up with boards. The kitchen had been tacked onto the south side of the cabin.

"What a great surprise!" exclaimed Rachel. "You have a new cook stove."

"That's not the surprise," chorused the giggling children.

"My neighbor, Palmer Helgren gave me the stove," explained Sadie. "He and his friend Eli set it up."

"Do you know Eli?" asked Ruth.

"I do." The mention of Eli's name warmed Rachel's heart. His gentle strength was as impressive as his looks."

"He's strong," piped up David. "He chopped wood for us."

"Palmer made these benches for us," said Sarah proudly. "Now we ain't sittin' on the floor no more."

"Palmer likes us," said little Rachel with a big grin.

"Eli is our friend, too," added Leah.

Sadie added more wood to the stove. She poured water into her cast iron skillet and added some salt. "Oscar traded apples for oats, flour and cornmeal."

"We got lots of apples," nodded Leah.

Lydia added, "We make applesauce, but it's sour cuz we ain't got no shuger."

"Sadie let me make the oatmeal," offered Rachel pushing Sadie into the only kitchen chair. "You look so bone weary, way too pale and thin. Are you still nursing the twins?"

"I'm trying to wean them," said Sadie with a weary sigh, resting her arms on the swelling mound of her unborn child.

"Sadie, how did you get those bruises on your arms?"

Silence fell over the house like a heavy fog. Sadie wore a blank, hopeless stare like a bird caught in a snare. Remembrance of the horrors she had lived through rushed over her like a tidal wave. Sadie took a deep shuddering breath. Her downcast eyes were brimming with tears. Tremors of fear and desperation overtook Sadie's careworn body and she shook with shuddering sobs as deep as a bottomless chasm.

Rachel bent over and wrapped her arms around the delicate weeping body with tender sympathy.

David exploded angrily, "Papa ties her to the bedpost!"

Sarah spoke up next, "Papa is mean when he drinks too much licker!"

"We skairt!" cried little Rachel.

Rachel felt her uncharitable thoughts toward Oscar growing like a blazing prairie fire. Sadie's life was like an unmanageable ball of knots, too tangled to understand. Rachel silently cried out for answers. How could she help Sadie? Sadie pushed golden strands of wet hair away from her face with her work-worn hands. She wiped the tears from her emerald green eyes with her apron.

"Are you okay Mama?" asked Ruth gently.

Sadie nodded gravely.

"Mama, can we show Miss Rachel our surprise now?" asked David.

"Of course," said Sadie with a quivering voice. "LIne up, I'll get my spoon."

The children grouped together as if they were getting ready for a photograph. Older ones in the back row, stair-stepping down to the youngest.

Sadie took her wooden spoon and started tapping out the tune on her kitchen table. The children's voices blended in perfect harmony as they sang: *"Round and round the cobbler's bench, the monkey chased the weasel. The monkey thought 'twas all in fun when POP goes the weasel!"* The twins, Joel and Jonathan popped up a little late. The older children were almost finished with the 2nd verse.

Rachel applauded loudly! "I'm so impressed. You are all so musical! **Encore, encore!**"

The children shrugged their shoulders and stared in wonder.

Sadie explained, "Rachel wants more music." She picked up her spoon and tapped out the next tune and they sang: *"A farmer's dog sat on the porch and Bingo was his name. BINGO, BINGO, BINGO, and Bingo was his name..."*

"Bravo!" shouted Rachel. Then an idea popped into her head. "Larson's have free puppies. Do you want me to bring you one?"

David shook his head, "can't have a dog."

Sadie explained with sadness in her voice, "Oscar hates dogs! We can't have one. Oscar would kill it!"

"I'm so sorry," apologized Rachel.

"It's okay, we have Tabby," piped up Leah.

Lydia added, "she can stay, cuz she catch mice."
"Mama ain't got a p'ano, that's why she plays with a spoon," explained David.
Lydia spouted, "she ain't got fiddle ether."
Leah her twin chimed, "Mama can sing like the birds."
"She got music in her head," added little Rachel proudly.
Sadie explained, "My mother, my sister and I had many students. We taught piano, violin and guitar lessons."
Rachel was grateful that Sadie seemed to be remembering more and more details with each visit. "That was a good source of income."
"Yes, but we never saw any of the money. My father was in charge of that, but I still loved my job. Father was a talented fiddle player when he wasn't drinking. But he didn't have the patience to teach lessons like we did."
Rachel's heart was sobbing silently. History had a way of repeating itself. First a drunk for a father and now one for a husband. She offered up a prayer of help for Sadie. "Well, I have a surprise for you, too."
The children followed Rachel like ducklings in a row.
Rachel pulled a package out of her saddlebag and announced, "sugar for the applesauce."
The children clapped their hands.
Rachel took another large bag of the saddle-horn. "I found some clothing and shoes that might fit you and the children in the Share Box at the office.
The children ran to get apples and filled Rachel's saddle bags. Rachel graciously accepted the gift of apples. She remembered Jesus words at Acts 20:35, "There is more happiness in giving then there is in receiving." Sadie and her children needed every ounce of happiness they could find. Rachel mounted her horse and looked down on Sadie's smiling children. They were Sadie's pride and joy. The only thing she had in all the world. "You are all so beautiful just like your mother," praised Rachel.
Sadie treasured Rachel's kind words and stored them in an empty place in her broken heart.

Chapter 10   The Picnic

The day of the picnic finally arrived. Alice put on her new dress. The full sweep skirt in the wildflower print was attached to a lavender empire bodice. The sleeves made from the print were trimmed with scalloped lavender cuffs. The scoop neck and hemline were delicately scalloped. Alice had made a new band for her wide-brimmed sun hat with a scrap of the wildflower print. She hurried downstairs and found Tobia washing Ardis face and hands.
"Ta-da!" giggled Alice spinning around with her flowing skirt.
"Ante Alice you luk purtee," spouted Ardis.
Tobia nodded, "Ye luk lov'ly. Dat dres' is byutifel!"
"Oogah! Oogah!" Palmer blasted the Klaxon.
Ardis jumped up and down. "Lizzie is comin'!"
"Vho dat be?" blurted Tobia.
Palmer was cruising up the Hoversten lane with his new dark green Ford C-cab. They all rushed out on the front porch. Ed came strolling from the barn as Palmer pulled his new truck to a stop.
"Vhen ye git dat goodt lukin' truck?" asked Ed overflowing with excitement.
"Yesterday, Eli took me to the Ford Motor Company in Mason City."
"It luks bran' nu," spouted Ed.
"It is, they didn't have any used ones."
"Dis is yust vhat ve need!" shouted Ed. "Tobia com' luk at dis truck!"
Palmer's gaze went to the front porch. There stood beautiful Alice in a lavender dress that showed off her graceful feminine curves. His heart leaped with a rush of excitement.
"Picnic!" cried Ardis as he ran toward Palmer.
Palmer tossed him up in the air and the little fellow squealed with giggles. Ardis loved rough play!
Alice stared at Palmer. He looked so handsome in his light blue shirt and new denim jeans. His tanned face glowed in the sun and his wind-blown wavy hair fell down on his forehead in disarray. This dashing young fellow always seemed to send Alice's butterflies fluttering out of control.
"I'll get the picnic basket," called Alice returning to the kitchen.
Ardis scrambled into the truck, "Ready!"
"He alvays rede to go," chuckled Tobia.
Palmer met Alice at the steps. They stared into each other's eyes, savoring the moment as long as possible.

Ed whispered, "Dose two mak' handsom' kupl'."
"Von't be long, lov' in da air," agreed Tobia.
Ardis waved good-bye as the Ford truck cruised down the lane with the summer breeze blowing through their hair.
"Is dis truck named Lizzie?" asked Ardis.
"No," laughed Palmer. "I'm thinking about naming it Henry."
"Why you do that?" asked Ardis.
"Because Henry Ford invented the first motorcar."
"He did," chimed Ardis.
Alice added, "I think Henry would be honored to have Palmer's first truck named after him."
"Well, Henry it is then," stated Palmer.
"Where we go?" asked Ardis.
"It's a surprise," teased Palmer. "You'll see soon."
"Gamma say I a shaperon, but dun't 'no' what it is," said Ardis with a baffled look.
Alice explained, "It's a person who goes along with an unmarried couple on a date."
"Are we on a date?" asked Ardis.
"Yes, our picnic is a date," giggled Alice.
"How old are you Ardis?" asked Palmer in amazement.
Ardis held up two fingers.
"You are the smartest two year old I know!" exclaimed Palmer.
"He'll be three in December," reported Alice.
Palmer asked, "How did you get so smart?"
Ardis shrugged his shoulders, "What is smart?"
"Palmer it's your turn," giggled Alice.
Palmer explained, "You're smart because you know a lot for a two year old."
"Is smart good?" asked Ardis.
"It's your turn Alice," laughed Palmer.
"Ja, Ardis, smart is very good!"
Ardis started to sing, *"Pop goes the weasel..."*
"We're almost there," informed Palmer stopping on the bridge, so they could look down into the slowly moving creek.
"Is dere fish in dere?" asked Ardis.
"Lots of bullheads, carp, turtles, crawfish, frogs and an occasional harmless water snake," laughed Palmer.
"I don't like snakes," confessed Alice. "But I would like to go fishing sometime."

"Me too," chimed Ardis.

Palmer turned into his long driveway. Evergreens grew on both sides of the lane. The homestead sat on a hill above a wooded creek valley. To the west was a large white barn. The big two-story house had stately gables trimmed in gingerbread and a big country porch with matching porticoes. In the front yard was a weeping willow tree and a large oak from which a swing hung. A big golden retriever came around the side of the house barking loudly, but at the same time wagging his tail. When he saw Palmer, he bolted toward his master.

"Howdy Max," greeted Palmer. The dog raised his paw to shake Palmer's hand. "Meet Alice and Ardis." Max extended his paw to shake hands.

"He smart," spouted Ardis.

Palmer picked up a stick and threw it. "Fetch, Max!" The dog returned with his stick, but refused to surrender it to his master.

"He is really smart," agreed Alice. "He worked for that stick and now he's going to keep it."

Ardis ran to the swing, "p'eas'," he begged.

Palmer lifted him into the swing and gave him a push.

"Palmer you have a large garden."

"Well I can't take all the credit. I only till it in the spring and plow it in the fall. Mother and my sisters' plant, weed and harvest."

"How many brothers and sisters do you have?"

"I'm the oldest, then Clarence, Mabel, Hazel, Myrtle and Leonard. Helen Margaret was the baby. She got sick and never recovered," Palmer's voice cracked. He took a deep breath. "She's buried in the Rosehill Cemetery in Thompson." A silent sob escaped from deep within Palmer's heart.

Alice wished she knew what to say to ease Palmer's pain. "I'm so very sorry," whispered Alice with a voice full of gentle sympathy.

She struggled to overcome waves of emotion as her eyes brimmed with tears. Alice reached up to give Palmer a hug. Her gentle touch sent shivers through him. Palmer drew Alice into his arms and she leaned against his muscular chest. This extraordinary woman had a way of comforting his battered heart. He drew strength from her embrace. She was everything he ever needed. He wanted nothing more than to spend the rest of his life with her. Alice felt Palmer rest his chin on the top of her head. She felt so content and secure engulfed in his sturdy arms. His touch sent prickles running along her skin. The tender bud of love was starting to bloom in her heart. Alice and Palmer stood under the oak tree wrapped in an invisible strand of love. Two hearts entwined like kindred spirits.

No words were exchanged. No words were needed. Alice felt someone pulling on her dress.

"Ante Alice, gotta go!"

"Ardis, can you go behind the tree?"

"Okie dokie," Ardis skipped off with Max at his heels.

Palmer slowly released his embrace. "Our little chaperone is doing his job, so would you like to see the house?"

"I'd love to see it. Ardis c'mon!"

The front porch looked so inviting. A wooded porch swing made of cedar hung on one side of the front door. On the other side were two straight-back chairs and a small table. A sign saying "Home Sweet Home" hung by the door. Palmer Opened the screen door and they stepped into a big parlor. The house had polished oak floors. The top of the walls were wallpapered in a blue striped pattern. The bottom had wainscot matching the woodwork. The room had a blue sofa with a matching chair and a small round table. On the table lay Palmer's Bible next to a kerosine lamp.

"This door goes to a bedroom. I guess it was used as a nursery."

"What's a nersere?" asked Ardis. Alice answered, "It's a room for babies and children like you."

"Member, I a big broder now!" reminded Ardis.

A wide door took them into a large dining room which was empty except for a two-drawer Shaker desk and a small bookcase. Above the desk hung a desk organizer with three drawers and lots of cubbyholes. On top of the desk lay Palmer's black ledger. They entered a small hallway and Palmer opened a door to another empty room.

"I think this would make a nice lavatory someday."

Ardis asked, "What's laventore?"

"It's an inside outhouse," grinned Palmer.

To the left was a staircase.

"There's three bedrooms and attic storage up there."

The next door took them into Palmer's bedroom. It had a walk-in-closet under the stairs and another door to get back to the nursery. The room had a walnut four-poster bed and a matching bureau. A looking glass hung above it.

"This is a log cabin pattern," said Alice looking at the patchwork quilt on the bed.

"I've had that quilt since I was a boy. It's thin and threadbare like an old sock, but I still love it."

"A person can't put a price on something that's attached to precious memories," called Alice's sweet voice.

They followed Palmer back through the dining room and into the kitchen. It had a small square butterfly table with four chairs. The cupboards were white and the one next to the dry-sink had glass doors. Alice could see Palmer's speckled blue enamel dishes, a coffee pot, plates, cups and bowls. It had an ice-box and a shiny black cook-stove. On the wall hung a cast iron skillet with a matching lid.

"Your stove looks new!" said Alice tucking away a smile.

"It is," said Palmer. "I don't know how to cook. I gave the old stove to Sadie, Oscar's wife. The poor woman was still cooking in the fireplace."

The sink sat below a window that looked out to a small herb garden.

Ardis asked, "What dat door do?"

Palmer opened the pantry door and Alice and Ardis peeked in.

"Gamma calls pantre spiskammer, dat's wegian," explained Ardis.

Just inside the door set a white porcelain enameled pail with a matching lid and water dipper. It was used for drinking and cooking water carried from the well. The shelves were lined with Mason canning jars full of vegetables, fruit, pickles and jam.

"Palmer did you can all this food?"

"Oh, sure I did," laughed Palmer. "The truth is I'm indebted to Mother and my sisters."

There were cans of tea, coffee, sugar, flour, baking powder, salt, a glass bottle of vinegar and a can of lard. On the wall hung a popcorn popper, colander and a sieve. Next to the breadbox was a coffee grinder and an earthenware cookie jar.

"Mother keeps me in cookies. Let's see if she has been here." Palmer lifted the lid and peeked inside. "Well, someone has been here. There were three cookies left in that jar this morning. Now they're gone."

"Cookie thief!" cried Ardis.

"It looks that way. That's so strange, why would Mother take them? She's the one who fills the jar; I'm the one that empties it. Maybe my sisters are playing a joke on me. Three sisters and three cookies, mystery solved."

The kitchen led to a small entryway with a washstand, a pitcher and bowl. A homespun cotton towel hung over the back towel rack. The room had rows of hooks for hats and jackets. Another door led to the cellar. Near the back porch was a small shed. Palmer called it the bath-house. Inside was a galvanized tin tub and a small stove for heating the water. A shelf on the wall held towels and soap.

"Go on picnic now!" pouted Ardis.

"I have the perfect spot," said Palmer lifting the picnic basket out of the truck box. They walked down the lane toward the woods enjoying the sunshine and gentle breeze. Shadows were long and lazy at the edge of the woods. They entered onto a little-used path threading their way through the thick trees. Ardis followed Palmer like a noonday shadow. Green leaves made a canopy roof over their heads with bits of blue sky peeking through. The woods were full of wild strawberries, gooseberry and blackberry bushes.

"Is dere bears in here?" asked Ardis cautiously looking around.

"No, but we might see some birds, squirrels and rabbits. There's a Great Horned owl who lives out here and I've seen wild turkeys, too." Palmer stopped, "listen, it's the call of a bob-white." He whistled the same notes back in answer. A few seconds later the bob-white's whistle returned ringing through the woods.

"You talk to birds?" asked Ardis.

"If you can whistle you can," answered Palmer.

"I dunno how to whis-o, but Ante Alice does."

Palmer stopped under a huge, old cottonwood tree. Its silvery trunk was tall and stately, its boughs spreading far and wide heavily laden with leaves of green.

"Every time I come to the woods, I stop and stare at this tree in awe. I wonder how old it is. If only it could talk. Did the Indians sit in the shade off this grand old tree? Or was it just a sapling when the pioneers passed through here with their wagon trains. Did children play under its branches while their mothers washed clothes in the creek? How many storms has it battled? How many birds has it sheltered? Only its Creator knows!"

Alice added, "One thing is for sure, this majestic tree has seen many seasons come and go."

They passed elm, ash and maple trees. Palmer stopped to point out a yellow and black Tiger Swallowtail butterfly resting on Queen Anne's lace. Just then, Alice tripped over a big, shallow tree root. Palmer reached out and grabbed her hand. Alice heart leaped at his touch. Their fingers intertwined and so did their hearts.

"I'm so sorry," apologized Palmer. "I forgot to warn you about the tree roots. Are you okay?" he asked with tender concern.

"I'm fine," giggled Alice. "Looks like, I'm falling head over heels for you."

Palmer had to stomp down the desire to kiss her. It wouldn't be proper to be so forward and Ardis was sure to tell. He reluctantly let go of her hand. They reached a sunny hollow down in a clump of birch trees and could now hear the sweet song of the creek. Palmer set the picnic basket down.

"This is my thinking log. It's a great place to sit and enjoy nature. I like to meditate on all my blessings. This secluded place is quiet and devoid of distractions."
Ardis asked, "What is distrakshen?"
"You are a distraction," laughed Palmer. "Let's go skip rocks."
The clear creek ran in ripples, sparkling and tumbling along over the rocks, churning up little bubbles of foam. A gentle breeze ruffled the water and the sun drew diamonds across the surface.
"It's so beautiful here! I feel like I'm in a painting," said Alice gently.
Palmer thought her voice sounded as musical as the flowing creek. "Would you like to sit on my throne?" asked Palmer pointing at his fishing stump surrounded by feathery ferns. "You can be Queen of the Forest today."
"It would be my pleasure to sit on such a grand chair." Alice sat down on the fishing stump and her heart cried out with boundless joy.
Palmer threw a stone, skipping it across the water.
"Ante Alice, did you see that?" cried Ardis.
Queen Alice answered from her throne, "I did! It skipped all the way across the creek."
Ardis threw his stone and it made tiny circles in the water. "Dis is fun! I do it agin!"
"Are you getting hungry?" asked Alice.
"Of course, I'm starving," grinned Palmer.
"Me too," agreed Ardis.
"I'll get things ready," announced Alice. She spread an old linen tablecloth on the ground in front of Palmer's thinking log.
Palmer and Ardis came racing back!
"My, you men must be hungry," said Alice trying to stifle her giggles.
"Ja, we're starving," stated Palmer. "We washed our hands in the creek."
"We all clean," said Ardis proudly holding up his little hands and Palmer mimicked Ardis showing his rough callused hands.
They all sat down in a circle and joined hands. Palmer prayed: "Heavenly Father, Sovereign Lord of the universe, we humbly approach your throne of undeserved kindness. You alone deserve our praise for you created all things and because of your will they exist. Your heavens declare your glory, your power, wisdom and love. Your invisible qualities are seen in your creation from the mighty cottonwood tree to the tiniest violet. Your wonders surround us with the music of the babbling brook, the scent of a pine tree, the beauty of a butterfly, the songs of your birds. We thank you for this day of life and the food set before us. Please

forgive us for our sins and deal mercifully with us, remembering that we are made of dust. You have showed us the greatest love that could ever be, by giving the life of your beloved Son, Jesus Christ. It's in his name that we offer this prayer. Amen."

It was hard for Palmer to let go of Alice's hand. He wanted to hold it forever. Alice knew that she had met the love of her life, but did Palmer feel the same way?

"Let's eat before the ants get it all," commanded Palmer.

"I smack 'em!" offered Ardis.

"Ardis has a plan to save us from the ants," giggled Alice filling plates with fried chicken, baked beans, buttermilk biscuits with strawberry jam.

"Oh, Alice! This is so good!" praised Palmer.

"Save room for cherry pie," advised Alice. "How did you find this wonderful place?"

"Max and I were chasing a runaway calf. I'm grateful that little fellow got out!"

"Do you have cattle?"

"Twenty beef cows, twelve calves, two draft horses, my black gelding, Pepper, two hogs and some chickens. Oh, and of course Max. Alice, tell me about your family. Have I met everyone?"

"Just about," explained Alice. "I have two older sisters. They were both born in Norway. Anna was ten years old when they came to America. She married Michael Risa in 1911. They have a farm in Hanley Falls, Minnesota. They have five children, Amy, Olaf, Thelma, Elmer and Mildred. My other sister, Inger was seven years old when they left Norway. She married Hawkin Berven in 1912. They farm northeast of Thompson. They just adopted the two children that were saved out of that tragic fire this spring. Allen is two years old."

"Like me," piped up Ardis.

"Ja, you're about two months older than Allen. His little sister Eunice is almost one. It's a miracle they survived. In fact, the neighbors who rescued them thought they were dead. They laid them on the corncob pile. The fresh air must have revived them and they started to cough. Hawkin and Inger attached themselves to those children like fleas on a dog."

"Let's play hide-and-seek," begged Ardis.

"Okay, you two hide and I'll find you," nodded Palmer. "I'll count to twenty. Better hurry! Run like the dickens! **ONE! TWO! THREE!...**"

Alice grabbed Ardis hand and hurried in the direction of the big cottonwood tree. They hid on the back side of the immense tree.

"TWENTY!" yelled Palmer. **"Ready or not here I come!"** He headed for the cottonwood tree knowing it would make a great hiding place.
Ardis peeked around the tree.
"Get back here," whispered Alice. "He'll see you."
As Palmer got closer he sang, *"Oh, where, oh where can they be?"*
Ardis jumped out, "Here I am!"
"Gotcha!" snapped Palmer as he grabbed Ardis and tossed him in the air. Ardis was breathless with excitement as he wiggled to get away.
Alice came out from behind the tree. "Here I am!" she said mimicking Ardis.
"Little boy, you are an endless source of amusement."
Palmer took great pains not to stare at Alice's radiant face. But the sight of her stirred up feelings within him. Laughter danced in her big, brown eyes. He had found a precious jewel of high value.
Alice was captivated once again by Palmer's blue eyes and irresistible smile. His face sparkled with laughter. She loved his sense of humor. In fact, she loved everything about this man.
Palmer carried the sleepy boy back to the thinking log.
"He's out," giggled Alice, "we have a sleeping chaperone."
"The poor little fellow has played himself out." Palmer's voice had a gentle tone.
"Palmer lead the way, I'll carry the picnic basket."
Palmer laid the sleeping child on Alice's lap. They headed down the lane in Henry, Palmer's new truck.
"Who planted the pink hollyhocks growing by the mailbox?" asked Alice.
"The birds did."
The events of the day flitted through Alice's mind. Alice knew she would treasure these precious memories forever. "I had an absolutely wonderful day and it's all because of you."
"I felt like I was living in a dream today," said Palmer with aching tenderness. "But if that were true, I'd never want to wake up."
Palmer spoke with such tenderness; Alice thought her heart would burst. His strong fingers wrapped around Alice's small hand. They held hands enjoying the solitude of the moment as they sped along over dirt roads leaving a cloud of dust behind.

Chapter 11   Female Fuss

The day was winding down and the sunlight was rapidly fading. The changing light began to bathe the porch with evening shadows. Palmer sat down on the porch swing with Max lying at his feet. He tried to recall the events of the day. Palmer didn't want to forget anything, not even the smallest details. It had been a perfect first date. Max's ears perked up. Palmer heard the hum of an engine. He reached down and patted the dog on the head. "It's okay Max. It's our friend Eli."...

"Sorry to come out so late," apologized Eli. "How did the picnic go?"

"We had a great time! Our little chaperone fell asleep, so I took them home. Is everything okay Eli? You look worried."

"I am!" Eli started pacing back and forth across the porch. His lofty stature cast long shadows like a mighty tree. "I feel like... I don't know how to...I mean..."

"Eli just spit it out."

"What I'm trying to say is, I'm down right plumb crazy about Rachel Allison. Palmer I feel like I've found honey in a bee hive, but now I don't know how to rob It."

"Eli it sounds like you're a goner."

"Ja, of course I am! Just like water under the bridge, I'm way beyond return. The problem is I just don't know anything about courtin' a woman. I'm supposed to woe her, right? Well I'm the one who's woozy! The whole thing boggles my mind. I don't know if she even likes me. I mean, what would a beautiful woman like Rachel see in a big ol' oaf like me? I don't know what to do next. I need some advice. Palmer how do I know what she's thinkin'?"

"You don't. Eli I'm new at this, too. I'm trying to figure it out as I go."

"Oh, great! That sounds like a no-fail plan. Well tell me, how did you get enough courage to ask Alice for a date?"

"I didn't," replied Palmer. "Ardis did it for me. He came right out and asked me if I was going to marry his Aunt Alice. That broke the ice."

"How old is that little fellow?" queried Eli.

"He's two."

"He's a smart one! I think I need to borrow that boy. Palmer, how come a two year old knows how to charm women and we don't?" Eli stopped pacing long enough to shake his head. "I'll tell you what I do know, Palmer. All this female fuss is sure a lot harder than threshing wheat!"

"Amen to that!" agreed Palmer.

"There's more," continued Eli. "Doc came down to the Blacksmith Shop today. He said Rachel had been out to see Sadie. Rachel's worried Sadie is runnin' on pure exhaustion. Thin as a rail, pale and all bruised up. David told Rachel that Oscar tied Sadie to the bedpost. Sarah claims Oscar has a mean streak when he's full of liquor. Palmer, what are we goin' to do? Do you think that cranky ol' coot will hurt those children?"

"I don't know," shrugged Palmer. "I've worried about it for years. Look how Oscar treats Sadie. He treats his mules a whole lot better. I would have sent Oscar packin' a long time ago, but I keep him on for the sake of Sadie and the children. I don't know what good it's doing if Oscar's spending his paycheck on whiskey."

"Palmer remember the day we set up the cook-stove for Sadie."

"Ja, why?"

"It was hot as the blazes that day! Why would a person wear a long skirt, long sleeve shirt, a scarf on her head on such a hot day? I'll tell you why? Sadie was covering up her battered body. And that explains why Oscar forbids her and the children from leaving the farm. He doesn't want anyone to know he beats her and he's afraid the children might slip and say something."

"Eli, have you ever thought about becoming a defense lawyer?"

"Well Palmer, the evidence is crystal clear. Even a nearsighted nincompoop could figure this one out. It's as sure as the green moss that always grows on the north side of a tree."

So Eli, what can we do?"

"I don't know it just doesn't make any sense. Why would a young beauty like Sadie marry a stubborn ol' buzzard like that?"

"Maybe, she didn't have a choice. Oscar told me he had traded his best mule for Sadie. He claims Sadie is his property and he'll do whatever he pleases with her. Sadie is hopelessly trapped in a precarious situation, shackled by an ignorant, cruel husband. It's a life of drudgery and I see no way out."

"That weasel is about as worthless as they come," agreed Eli. "He struts around like a cocky rooster braggin' about another child on the way. He doesn't deserve a family. He came in the Blacksmith Shop wearing a new shirt, trousers and boots. He says, 'ain't these boots a dandy!' I almost spit on them. His children are at home barefoot and wearin' rags. That two-timin' hypocrite is the only one in that family with shoes and a winter coat."

"You know Eli, Oscar's not very smart."

"You can say that again! Give the ol' horse-face enough rope and he's bound to hang himself."

"Eli let's keep mulling this over. Sleep on it and see if we can come up with a plan."
"Ja, there's got to be some way to outwit him."
"In the meantime, I'll try to work the tar out of him. Hard work might take the strut out of that cocky ol' rooster."

Chapter 12   Starry Night Sky

Alice's heart ached to see Palmer again. She replayed the day of the picnic over and over in her mind. It was all etched clearly in her memory. She had felt pure unhindered joy wrapped in Palmer's strong arms. Alice contemplated the possibilities in her heart. She dreamed about living in Palmer's house. Sewing curtains for the windows, polishing the oak floors, while the house filled with the smell of her fresh baked bread. Alice saw herself soaking in the big tub in the bathhouse after a hard day of work in the garden. Sitting next to Palmer on his thinking log down in his wooded retreat surrounded by the wonders of nature. Was it all just a dream? It seemed too wonderful to be true. Yet hope fluttered in her heart. Alice tried to stay busy. She helped Ed with the chores morning and evening. Alice helped Tobia keep the canner going, stocking up food for winter. There were clothes to wash and hang out on the line. She had almost finished her sewing job for Eli. Alice had made him three pairs of denim trousers and a stack of shirts. In the evenings she sat on the front porch making buttonholes and sewing on buttons until the night shadows closed around her. Alice stared into the starry heavens, deep and unfathomable. The stars looked like sparkling jewels. Was Palmer staring at the same stars, where ever he was? The days dragged on. Why didn't he come? Where was the man with the sky-blue eyes and captivating smile? The man who always stirred her butterflies into a flutter. Alice eyes clouded with tears. Were her hopes and dreams just a fleeting moment in the endless stream of time? She tried to calm her anxious heart, but there was nothing there but emptiness.

~~~~~~

Alice's beauty, her laughter, her musical voice all hung in the rafters of Palmer's mind. Memories of her big, brown eyes melted him completely like the puddle remaining of a snowman after a sunny day. Did those beautiful eyes hold secrets hidden from him? How could he know if Alice felt the same way? Did her heart leap for joy at the sight of him? Was her pulse racing like his? He remembered a glowing vision of Alice crossing the wheat field. She looked like a beautiful rare flower in a barren wilderness. The sun shone on her delicate face framed in her white sunbonnet. She wore that pretty brown dress with the tiny white daisies that swirled around her legs as she walked. Her graceful movements were like the fluttering of little white butterflies above the cucumber patch in his mother's garden. Palmer knew that as long as he lived, he would never forget the supple grace of Alice crossing that wheat field silhouetted in the sunshine. He had known on that day, at that very moment, that he had met the love of his life. He longed to see Alice, not just in his dreams, but every day for the rest of his life. It had taken a whole week to put up the hay and another full week of threshing, working until darkness over took them. He missed Alice so much, one evening he had gone down to his retreat in the woods. He sat alone on his thinking log, well not exactly. His faithful dog, Max lie at his feet. Palmer sat staring at the quiet grandeur of the starry night sky studded with glistening stars. Who caused the innumerable stars to stretch out across the vastness of space? Who sustains the stars through their endless cycles? What bonds hold the stars in place with spectacular precision? Palmer felt the vastness of the universe was truly beyond human comprehension! Thinking about it was awe-inspiring, yet he felt an inner peace. With renewed strength, he felt he could endure another day without seeing Alice. Was Alice staring at the same starry night sky? He believed she was and the thought gave him some comfort, yet he felt so utterly lonely.

Chapter 13   The Secret

Sadie used her whetstone to sharpen her scythe. She needed to start cutting the broomcorn. It would take several weeks to cure and many more to make the brooms. Sadie loved making brooms. It gave her great satisfaction knowing she was making a useful tool. She remembered her grandmother's favorite saying, "A new broom sweeps clean, but an old broom knows where the dirt is." The memory brought a needed smile to Sadie's weary face. Her grandparents had taught her everything she needed to know about broom making. Sadie's broom business brought in vital income for the Vage family. Oscar traded her brooms for supplies at the general store. Mr. Erickson had ordered a dozen sideliner brooms, used to sweep crumbs off tabletops and flour off breadboards. The order included two dozen whisk brooms, great for cleaning benches, hearths, clothing and stairways. The perfect tool for getting dust and cobwebs out of corners. Elias had also ordered six pot brooms used for cleaning kettles and pots. And one dozen long handle brooms handy for sweeping dirt and snow off sidewalks. Sadie was grateful for the order. There were so many things they needed. She had been out of baking powder for months and Oscar complained constantly about the flat biscuits. Sadie hoped there would be enough income to get the children coats and shoes for winter. The children longed to play in the snow, but many winters had come and gone and still they had no shoes.

Sarah was helping David do the morning chores. Ruth had spread an old threadbare quilt under the oak tree near the field of broomcorn where she seated the children. Ruth drew pictures in the dirt with a stick and her siblings tried to guess what she had drawn. Sometimes they needed a little help, so Ruth added sound effects and charades. Sadie felt Ruth was a very talented artist and she hoped to add paper and a pencil to the long list of needs.

Sadie's broomcorn was about five feet tall and each plant had a brushy tassel with a few dozen fibers about two feet long. Sadie walked backwards between two rows of broomcorn breaking the stalks so that they crisscrossed and formed a "table." Then she cut each brush off just below the crown and piled them in the V she had created by crisscrossing the stalks. Sadie carefully gathered the fibrous tassels by hand. She would thresh out the seeds and use them to plant next year's crop. The seedless stiff brush must be cured for several weeks. Extra care was taken to prevent the fibers from becoming tangled and broken. Later, the children would help Sadie separate the fibers according to length, quality and color. Sadie sang, "Beautiful Dreamer" as she worked and no meadow lark had ever sang more beautiful. Sadie's thoughts drifted back to her childhood. She remembered her mother's loving face and her soothing voice was always a comfort to Sadie and her sister. *Yes, I have a sister, we're twins. I'm sure that's right. Oh, why can't I remember her name? If only I had a Bible, I'm sure it was a Bible name. And how could I forget my own mother's name?* Sadie remembered her mother playing the piano and she had danced with her sister with boundless joy. Mother had taught her to play the piano, violin, guitar and banjo. Music was her life and she loved it. Sadie's father was known as one of the best fiddlers in the state. *What state? Where did I live?* Happiness danced in every corner of the house when they were making music together, but terror reigned when father was drunk. Sadie shuddered with thoughts of those dark memories.

David's voice shattered her thoughts, **"Mama, Mama, come quick!"**

Was someone hurt? She heard the voices of her children all talking at the same time. With a pounding heart, Sadie raced out of the field of broomcorn. The children surrounded David who stood in the middle beaming with excitement and in his hands he held a fiddle.

"Mama, look what I found hidden in the barn!"

Sadie stepped forward in disbelief as David handed her the fiddle.

"It's beautiful, of high quality! Why this looks just like the fiddle I had as a young girl."

"Mama, can you teach me to play?"

"Of course I can," answered Sadie trying to find her voice. *Or can I? Do I remember how to play?*

To Sadie's surprise, David planted a big kiss on his mother's cheek. "Mama, Miss Rachel is right. Kisses are good medicine," explained David.

Sarah and Ruth started to laugh and all the children followed until the field of broomcorn was filled with their happy laughter.

Suddenly a thought of terror struck Sadie. Her mind was racing! "Children come and sit down on the quilt."

Sarah recognized the fear in her mother's trembling voice and asked, "Is everything okay?"

"We need to talk," explained Sadie as they all sat down under the oak tree. "This is very important children, so please listen carefully. We cannot tell anyone that we found this fiddle. David's find must be kept a secret."

"But who does it belong to?" asked Ruth.

Sadie shook her head, "I don't know."

"But why would someone hide it in the barn?" questioned Sarah.

"I just don't know, it makes no sense! But the fact that they hid it means that they did not want it to be found. I'm sure it was hidden for a good reason."
David asked, "Mama, will Papa beat us if he finds out?"
Sadie shrugged her shoulders. *Surely there would be severe consequences to pay for this find. She was taking a huge risk! Would the risk be worth it? Sadie had longed to play for thirteen very long years. Could this be an answer to her prayers? Would the risk be worth it? Ja, it would be.*
Little Rachel broke the silence, "Mama, are ye dun thinkin'?"
"Ja, I'm done. David you must always put this fiddle back in its hiding place exactly the way you found it."
"It was in this black case," said Sarah holding it up.
"Don't worry Mama, I'll put it back just the way I found it," assured David.
"We'll even throw some dust on it," offered Sarah.
"Okay, let's get this fiddle tuned and do some real dancing. We'll play and sing and laugh and dance until we all drop!"
A mighty chorus of happy voices burst forth from Sadie's children!

Chapter 14   Cookie Thief Mystery

Martha picked up her telephone receiver and cranked the handle on the side. "Number please?" Karina Anderson was the telephone operator for King Telephone Company. She recognized every single customer by their voice.
"Karina, this is Martha Helgren speaking."
"Well Hello Martha! How is your family?"
"We are all fine. How are you?"
"I can't complain. The weather is sure nice for August. Not so hot like some years."
"Yes, the crops look wonderful from all this rain we've been blessed with."
"My parents are still talking about Palmer and his threshing crew. Father claims he has never seen anyone work so hard."
"Well Palmer has always believed that hard work is a gift from God."
"Well it certainly shows. So what number do you need, Martha?"
"I need the number for Edward and Tobia Hoversten, please."
"Just one minute, I'm pretty sure it's 36. Let me check the list. Yes, their number is 36. Would you like me to connect?"
"Yes, please do."
"Oh, Martha, please remind John the meeting for King Telephone Company this month is Tuesday evening at seven o'clock."
"I'll remind him, thanks Karina."
"Ring, Ring, R-i-n-g..."
"Two short and one long, that's our ring Mother!" hollered Alice from the back porch where she was churning butter.
"I git," returned Tobia. "Haloo!"
"Is this Tobia?" asked Martha.
Before Tobia realized it her Norwegian slipped out, "Jo, det er det! Sorre, I fergit som' tim'," she apologized.
"That's okay," consoled Martha sympathetically. "Both of my parents came from Norway, so I speak some Norwegian. My husband is from Sweden, so I speak a little of that, too. Tobia, the reason I'm calling is to invite you, Edward and Alice for dinner on Saturday."
"Ve lik' dat!" chimed Tobia.
"Good, we're looking forward to it, too. We eat at noon. My telephone number is 6 if you need to reach me. Ha det, Tobia."
"Mange takk! Ha det, Martha."

"Who was that Mother?" inquired Alice.
"Dat Martha Helgren. She vant us com' fer dinner on Saturday."
Hope fluttered in Alice's heart. It seemed an eternity since she had seen Palmer.
"What should we take?"
"Ve got but'ermilk. Kin mak' Kringla Kukes."
"Ja, and let's make lefse, too," suggested Alice. "Oh, Mother, I just can't wait!"

~~~~~~

The days crawled by, but finally Saturday arrived. After chores Alice took a bath and washed her hair rinsing it with rainwater mixed with rosemary. Tobia had cut her hair off at shoulder length. *What if Palmer doesn't like it?* Negative thoughts entered her mind and struggled to take over, but she refused to allow them any space. Alice put on her plum-rose dress with the folkloric embroidery. It had a matching bonnet that would keep her hair clean from the dusty roads.
Ed hitched up Nelly to the buggy and they were on the way.
"Do you know how to get there Father?" asked Alice with a worried tone.
"Dun't vorre," reassured Ed. "John tel' me how to git dere. It 'bout four mil'. Dere farm two mil' west of Thompson."
Alice waited with eager anticipation as Nelly plodded along.
"Ve 'bout dere!" announced Ed as he turned into the Helgren's lane.
Alice heart sank like the setting sun. Her greatest fear had just materialized. Palmer's Ford truck was not there and neither was Pepper, his black gelding. Her tiny flicker of hope was dead. Her butterflies exploded and lay in a heap in the pit of her stomach. Her thoughts and feelings were in turmoil, running free rein in her mind and heart. Alice knew she was on the verge of tears. She struggled to swallow and took a deep, shaky breath. The Helgren family was all standing on the front porch awaiting their arrival. What a grand display of hospitality. Why should Alice be surprised? She was sure they were just like Palmer. Alice knew she must return the same kindness. It was time to drag a smile out of her back pocket and paste it on her lifeless face.
"This is my youngest son, Leonard. He'll take care of your horse," offered John.
"Mange takk!" exclaimed Ed climbing out of the buggy.
John extended his hand to help Tobia and Alice down. "Welcome to our home, ladies. Martha, this is Tobia and Alice Hoversten."
Martha came down the porch steps and gave Tobia a big hug. As she hugged Alice she whispered, "Alice you look lovely."

Alice croaked out a, "thank you."

"These are our daughters," said John sweeping his arm toward the porch. Each stepped forward introducing themselves.

"I'm Mabel Josephine. I'm so glad to meet you!"

"I'm Hazel Jeanette. I feel like I already know you. Palmer talks of nothing else. It seems like I've waited forever to meet you."

Her younger sister interrupted, "I'm Myrtle Claretta and I think Hazel talks too much!"

Everyone exploded with laughter, except for Hazel.

Martha called, "Everyone come in and make yourself at home!"

"It smel' vonderful in here," praised Tobia.

Hazel peeked in Alice's basket. "Mother, there's Kringla and lefse in here. Oh, I'm so in love with that yummy stuff!"

"Stay out of there!" bossed Mabel. "That's dessert."

"Girls, let's get dinner on the table," reminded Martha.

"Your dress looks amazing Alice," said Myrtle with the same captivating smile as Palmer's. "Did you do the embroidery?"

"No, Mother did," said Alice as she removed her bonnet. "She learned the art of folkloric embroidery from her mother in Norway."

Mabel spoke up, "I'd love to learn to do that!"

"I kin show ye gerls," offered Tobia.

"Mother look at Alice's hair," chimed Hazel. "I want to cut my hair like that!"

Alice heard the hum of an engine. Her butterflies started to wake up and flutter. When Palmer stepped through the door, Alice's butterflies soared into perfect flying formation. Their eyes met and Palmer was drowning in Alice's eager gaze. There she stood his daisy in the wheat field. His emotions were whirling him about and sucking him under like a drowning sailor going down for the last time. The love bug was buzzing around like a honey bee intoxicated with nectar. Alice felt her heart was flying on wings. Her butterflies soared higher and higher.

Ed broke the silence, "long tim', no see." He gave Palmer a hearty handshake.

"Let's eat," suggested John as he herded everyone to the dining room table. Hazel shoved Palmer into a chair next to Alice. Everyone joined hands for prayer. Palmer's strong fingers wrapped around Alice's small hand and their hearts leaped with joy!

"Let us pray," said John. "Heavenly Father, Creator of heaven and earth, we humbly approach you. You alone are worthy of our praise and devotion. We pray for your wisdom and guidance in doing your will. Grant us our daily needs and protect us from the evil one. May we imitate you by forgiving one another freely. We thank you for the precious gift of family and true friends. May your Kingdom come and set all matters right. May your will be done on earth as it is in heaven. Help us to follow closely in the footsteps of your beloved Son. It is in Jesus name that we pray. Amen."

Amens echoed around the table.

"Where's Clarence?" asked Palmer looking around the room.

"He called and said one of his mares is about to foal. He didn't want to leave her," explained Martha.

"What part of Norway did you come from?" inquired John.

"Ve vuz raised on Rennesoy Island off the west coast of Norway. At Stavanger," explained Ed, "ye got to tak' ferre fourteen mil's to da main island."

"I bet it is really beautiful there," replied Martha.

Tobia answered, "Ja, vere byutifel. Ve mis' wintre Northern Lites."

John thinking back to his childhood stated, "The Northern Lights, the aurora borealis is unforgettable! The beautiful eery light it produces is etched in my memory forever."

Ed added, "Norway has much beaute, high mauntins vith snow on top, deep fjords, vaterfulls, forest, lak's and reindeer herds. But lit'l land to farm. John vere ye com' fram?"

"I was born in Ystad, Sweden. I came over in 1886, at the age of nineteen."

"Ye com' alon'?" asked Ed.

"Ja, it was very hard to leave. I left behind my folks, Peter and Bertha, my older brother Olaf, two sisters, Anna and Ida and my baby brother Nils. He was just three years old when I left."

"Ye a brave man John! Ve left behind famle, too. Our folks, broders, sisters, onkels and tantes. It vas touf trip acros' oshen! Tobia, Anna an' Inger all sesick. Ve vorre 'bout runnin' out of food."

"I remember," agreed John "couldn't wait to set foot on dry land again."

"Vhat ye do vhen ye git to Amarika?" asked Ed.

"The first thing I did was change my Swedish name. It was Johannes Anton Joseph Hellgren."

"So that's where I got my middle name, Joseph," piped up Leonard.

Martha nodded, "Leonard Joseph, that's where it came from."

John continued, "I dropped one of the l's in Helgren and took John for a first name. I was in a new country and wanted a new start. I settled near Forest

City, Iowa for a few years, and then worked for a dollar a day at the Brones farm. I had learned the trade of blacksmith from my Father."

Palmer added, "Besides farming and the Blacksmith Shop, he's assessor of King township, a member of the school board and secretary of King Telephone Company."

"Ye aur von buse felo John," chuckled Ed. "How much land ye got here?"

"160 acres," stated John.

Martha shook her head, "Now he's thinking about running for mayor."

"He be goodt at dat, too," complimented Ed.

"Everything is delicious!" exclaimed Palmer. "This is the best meal I've had since the picnic."

Tobia added, "I hav' to git y'r resip' fer dose Swedish meatbal's an' noodl's. It so goodt! Da best I ever hav'!"

"Mange takk, Tobia," replied Martha. "Palmer claims your lefse is excellent."

Palmer pleaded, "I was hoping you girls would fill my cookie jar."

"We did!" chorused Palmer's sisters.

Palmer lay down his fork and stared at them in disbelief. "I never found any cookies."

"We put them in your cookie jar, like always," stated Mabel.

"Do we need to refresh your memory," giggled Myrtle, "two kinds of cookies, sugar and oatmeal raisin."

Palmer shook his head.

"You didn't eat them in your sleep, did you?" teased Hazel.

"Did you find the loaf of bread in your breadbox?" questioned Mabel.

Martha added, "I left a big piece of cherry pie on your kitchen table along with some fresh churned butter for your bread. Surely you remember that."

Palmer shook his head, "I never found any of it!"

"Is anything else missing?" queried Martha.

Palmer shrugged, "Well, I'm not sure. I saved three cookies for the day of the picnic. When we peeked into the jar it was empty. I thought you girls were playing a joke on me. Three sisters, three cookies, I thought the mystery was solved."

"We didn't take them," confirmed Hazel.

"So I suppose you expect me to believe they grew legs and ran off like the gingerbread man," quipped Palmer.

"So what have you been eating?" asked Martha with concern.

"Not much," complained Palmer. "I ate boiled eggs for breakfast and I found a small watermelon in the garden that was ripe. I had a good meal at noon. We were putting up hay and threshing for the Jacobson, Serby and Pederson families. I didn't get home until dark. I was going to dig potatoes, but I couldn't find the shovel."

"Hoe is missing, too," reported Hazel. "I couldn't find it anywhere."

"You know what I did find," continued Palmer. "A piece of someone's trousers in the front yard. I think Max had a little tussle with someone."

Alice spoke up, "Maybe Max smelled the cookies in the thief's pockets."

"Ja, that makes sense," agreed Palmer. "Max would do anything for a cookie. I doubt if the thief got away with very many cookies. Come to think of it, Max didn't eat his supper that night. I bet his tummy was full."

"Wow! We've got a real detective case going on here," cried Hazel. "This will be my next story, 'The Cookie Thief Mystery'."

"I can't stand a dishonest man!" snapped John.

Ed nodded in agreement, "Amen to that!"

Palmer asked, "Which day did you leave the cookies?"

Martha looked at the girls for help, "Wasn't it on a Wednesday the first week? And I think a Thursday last week."

"That's right," agreed Mabel. "We dropped the food off on the way to the fair."

"Palmer, guess who won the pie-eating contest this year?" spouted Hazel.

"Who?"

"Oscar Vage, that's who!" exclaimed Hazel.

"It was disgusting," blurted Myrtle. "He kept belching, but stuffed more in."

"He eats like a vulture!" agreed Mabel.

Palmer said thoughtfully, "Well, that explains why he missed work on Thursday."

"Does he miss a lot of work?" asked Leonard.

"Ja, he's always got some complaint." Palmer tried to mimick Oscar, *"I-a hurtin' in mi side. I gots a headach! Lookee, I git blister! Mi vife dun't do a lick of vork. I gots to do it all!"*

A titter of laughter broke out around the table.

Martha changed the subject. "Do you get the 'Old Farmer's Almanac'?"

"Nei, kin't re'd to goodt in englis'," admitted Tobia.

Martha explained, "Well there's a quote in there from 1891. I'm thinking about making a sign to hang in my kitchen. It said: *'The man who cannot eat his wife's over-baked bread without complaining, ought to be compelled to cook his own food until he mends his manners.'"*

Tobia started to chuckle, "I needs von of dose fer mi kitshun."

"Every woman should have one," spouted Mabel.

More laughter, but not so much from the men.

"Alice, do you want to play Croquet?" asked Hazel.

"I'm not sure what that is," admitted Alice.

"It's a yard game," explained Hazel. "We ordered it by mail from Montgomery Ward catalog. No one is sure who invented this ancestral game. Some claim it was introduced to Britain from France during the reign of Charles II of England in 1630. Others claim it came from Ireland."

Palmer laughed, "As you can see, Hazel is our walking encyclopedia."

"Very funny, Palmer!" Hazel continued, "the game of Croquet took England by storm in the 1860's and then spread overseas."

Alice asked, "How do you play?"

Hazel explained, "the game was at first called pall-mall from the Latin words for ball and mallet. You use your mallet to hit your ball through the wickets, hoops, kind-of like a horseshoe stuck in the ground."

"I'll go set it up," offered Leonard.

"I want the red," claimed Myrtle.

Hazel protested, "Alice is our guest, she should choose first. There's black, red, green, blue, orange and yellow."

"I'll try the green," replied Alice.

"Blue for me," added Palmer.

After the dishes were done the adults watched from the front porch.

Hazel reported, "Alice has won almost every game. She is so good at this!"

"She's good at everything she does," assured Palmer.

"Next time we play, I want the green ball," complained Myrtle. "This red ball has a mind of its own!"

"That won't do any good," laughed Leonard.

Mabel agreed, "my orange ball has an ornery streak today, too!"

"Ve bet'er head fer hom'," sighed Ed. "It's 'bout chore tim'."

"Can Alice stay for supper?" begged Hazel. "We can take her home with Palmer's truck."

Palmer added, "I've got to run into town to buy some locks for the house and the tool shed. So we'll bring her home from there."

"Dat be find, but no spoonin' on da porch tonite," chuckled Ed.

Chapter 15   The Love Bug

After the supper dishes were done, Palmer, Alice and Hazel headed into Thompson.
"I want to sit by the window," cried Hazel. She was making sure Alice would be sitting next to Palmer. After all, it wouldn't hurt to help the Love Bug out just a little.
Palmer pulled up in front of Kelso's Hardware Store. "I'll be back in a few minutes and then we'll have a soda pop at the drugstore."
"It's kind-of late," implied Alice, "won't they be closed by now?"
"The Johnsons live up above the store," informed Hazel. "If no one's downstairs, you just ring the bell."
Palmer was side-swiped by Gyda Yawnson before he could reach the store. She came charging at him full rein.
"Yoo-hoo! I've been looking high and low for you. I even went out to your house. My, my, you look handsome this evening. You know, there oughta be a law against men as handsome as you." Gyda moved a step closer and Palmer moved a step back. "You know, when I was out at your house, I just happened to notice there are no curtains in the windows. You've got a real nice place out there Palmer, but it just needs a woman's touch if you know what I mean." As Gyda reached out to touch Palmer he took another step backwards. "I know a girl that loves to measure, oh, I mean sew. Now what's her name? Oh, I think they call her Alice..."
Alice whispered to Hazel, "We'll never get rid of her. That woman grows roots and breaths right down your neck."
"Ja, that woman is on a man-hunt for a new husband," murmured Hazel. "Hey, I've got an idea. Reach over there and blast the Klaxon."
"Okay, here goes."
"Oogah!"
Gyda jumped teetering to regain her balance. This was Palmer's chance to escape and he disappeared into Kelso's store like a bolt of lightning! Gyda moved to the truck window to give the girls a tongue-lashing. "Land Sakes Alive! You scared the wits out of me! I suppose you girls think it's funny! Well, let me tell you that was downright rude of..." Gyda recognizing Alice stopped in mid-sentence. "Egads! What on earth are you doing here Alice?" Without waiting for an answer Gyda babbled on, "I'll tell you exactly what you are doing here! You are trying to date two men at the same time. I know what you're up too! Why you little two-timer!

Scarce as real men are and you think you need two, do you? Shame on you! I even offered to share. Dear, I hate to be the one to tell you this, but you are just a young, foolish girl! Palmer needs a mature, experienced woman with good common sense, not a worthless giggly girl like you!" Gyda stopped for a second to ask, "and who are you?"
"I'm Palmer's sister Hazel."
"Well I must say, you are an attractive girl like your brother. I guess your good looks come from your father. John's a mighty fine looking man for his age."
Bertina Fardel saved the day as she grabbed Gyda's arm, "C'mon, I've got something very important to tell you and it just can't wait!" They hurried off down the wooden boardwalk.
Hazel exclaimed, "Good riddance! Don't worry about that old wind-bag. If I had a hatpin, I'd poke her and knock the sails out of her. She doesn't stand a chance, because Palmer is head over heels in love with you."
"I'm not so sure," said Alice meekly.
"Haven't you noticed the way he looks at you? He only has eyes for you! He's been struck with Love Bug Fever for sure! Alice can I be your bridesmaid? I've always wanted to be one."
"Palmer hasn't even kissed me. I'm not sure he wants a wife."
"Nonsense, he needs you! Palmer is kind-of shy around women. I guess, I'll have to give him a little push. Did you know he calls you his daisy in the wheat field?
"He does?"
"Ja, and there's more."
"What do you mean Hazel?"
"Have you ever read the Song of Solomon?"
"Ja, it's one of my favorite books in the Bible."
"Well, that's how Palmer described you as a daisy 'among thorns' as his 'beloved'." Oh, Alice, it sounded so romantic, almost poetic. Oh, here he comes!"
As they walked to Johnson's Drug Store, Palmer thanked them for rescuing him from Gyda.
"Well good evening folks," greeted Ole Johnson as they sat down on bar stools near the fountain service.
"Ole when did you get electricity in here?" asked Palmer.
"Just got it installed last week. It's manufactured by the American Gas Company. You see those hollow copper tubes," said Ole pointing at the high tin ceiling.
"They carry gasoline under air pressure to the ceiling fixtures. The central gas tank is out back behind my store."

"It sure gives off a lot of light," remarked Palmer.
"It's real handy! I don't have to carry around Kerosene lamps now. My fountain clerk, Helga Huddelson has gone home for the day. I wonder if her apron will fit?" laughed Ole. "What can I get for you?"
"I'd like a Dr Pepper, please," ordered Hazel.
"That drink is really popular," explained Ole filling a glass from the tap. It was concocted in 1885 by a pharmacist named Charles Alderton of Waco, Texas. It didn't really become popular though, until it was introduced at the 1904 World's Fair in St. Louis, Missouri. After that the Dr Pepper fever swept the nation. I've got a new one. Do you want to try it?"
Palmer looked at Alice for approval.
"I've never had soda pop before," shrugged Alice.
"Never," said Ole, "well the first one's on the house." He poured three glasses from a bright green bottle called Green River. "It's got an intense lime flavor. What do you think?"
"It's very good," said Palmer waiting for Alice's reaction.
"I don't like it, I love it!" exclaimed Alice.
"Me too," said Hazel downing her glass. "I hope you sell it by the gallon."
"You think that's good," said Ole. "Try this!" He poured some Barqs soda into a glass and added a dip of ice cream and a spoon. "They call it a Root Beer Float, what will they think of next?"
When they came out of the drugstore the sun had rounded the corners of the earth.
"Looks like we'll need the lights," stated Palmer. He started the water drip into the carbide crystals of the head lamps, opened the lenses and lit the lamps. "We're ready to roll."
Dusk was quickly approaching as shadows of evening engulfed them. They watched the thin golden crescent of the moon rise in a darkening sky.
Palmer reached for Alice's hand lacing their fingers together. Alice rested her head on Palmer's shoulder. She was so full of contentment, she thought she might burst. The two miles to Alice's house sped by too quickly.
"I'll walk you to the door," offered Palmer as he helped Alice out of the truck.
"I forgot my bonnet," reported Alice.
"Good," said Palmer. "Now I have an excuse to come see you, again."
"You don't need an excuse. You're welcome any time."
"I had a wonderful day, Alice. It's always that way with you."
"Do you forgive me for beating you at the game of Croquet?"

"I do," laughed Palmer. "I love your lively spirited manner."

Hazel was coaching the Love Bug from Palmer's truck. "I'm counting on you to do your part little Love Bug," she whispered. "Palmer needs a little push; well you better make it a big push! In fact, the bigger the better!!!"

Palmer's dancing blue eyes gazed lovingly into Alice's beautiful brown eyes for a long time. He said nothing, but his intense gaze said more than words. His blazing heart was dancing like the wild flames of a fire again. Alice smelled so good. Her face was fine and delicate as a flower. Her cherry lips looked so soft and inviting. Palmer fought the urge to kiss Alice. He didn't want to overstep his bounds, but it was becoming more difficult. He knew he should go or a team of wild horses wouldn't be able to stop him. He stood there for ten more torturous seconds and then reluctantly pulled away.

"I had a wonderful time," came Alice's sweet voice like a spoken lullaby. "Thank you Palmer!"

"Good night my little daisy in the wheat field," came Palmer's gentle reply.

As Hazel saw Palmer coming down the walk she reprimanded the Love Bug, "I didn't see any sparks flying. Are you sleeping on the job? I was counting on you and you let me down!"

Palmer wheeled Henry around and started down the Hoversten's lane.

Hazel didn't waste any time. "So Palmer, did you kiss her?"

"Of course not! I didn't want to be too bold."

"Why not? You are head over heels in love with that girl. Are you waiting for the sky to fall?"

"Some chaperone you are, encouraging me to steal a kiss," retorted Palmer. "The truth is I've never kissed a girl before. I don't even know how."

"Well you better figure it out, soon! Palmer don't you get it? She's the one! The girl of your dreams! The capable wife of Proverbs chapter 31. 'Her value is far more than corals. She rises while it is still night providing food for her household. She plants a vineyard from her own labors. Her whole household is clothed in warm garments. She opens her mouth in wisdom. The law of kindness is on her tongue. The bread of laziness she does not eat.' Palmer, Alice is all of that and more. You have met the love of your life."

"I think she deserves better," said Palmer trying to arrange his thoughts.

"Nonsense, she needs you! Please take my advice. You, Palmer Olai Helgren have been bushwhacked by the Love Bug and you are way beyond the point of return. Surrender to the Love Bug!!!"

Chapter 16   My True Love Has My Heart And I Have His

Palmer woke up to the rumble of thunder. A flash of lightning lit the dark sky. A north-east wind was singing its humming tune. Another bolt of lightning zigzagged through the sky. "**FLASH! BOOM!**" The whole earth seemed to be vibrating! The pines along the lane bent to one another as if they were whispering secrets. The floodgates opened and the cloudburst showed no mercy.

~~~~~~

Palmer pulled his truck up to the Hoversten's barn. Ed was getting ready to hitch up the horses to haul his milk to the Thompson Creamery.
"Let's haul the cream cans in my truck," offered Palmer.
"Mange takk!"
"I heard Dr. Allison is selling his truck. I thought you might want to look at it."
"Did he git nu von?" questioned Ed.
"He bought a Stutz Bearcat. It sounds like a really sporty car."
They loaded the cream cans and headed into town.
Palmer was as nervous as a long-tail cat lying next to a rocking chair. He took a deep breath. He thought it would be best if he didn't beat around the bush. "Ed, I want to marry your daughter, Alice."
Ed chuckled, "Ye 'no' if ye tak' her, ye kin't bring her bak!"
Palmer's voice carried a hint of humor. "So you have a no-return-policy. That's okay, I was planning on forever, to death do we part."
"Wel' den ye hav' mi blessin'. I be proud to hav' ye fer son-in-law."
Relief burst through Palmer. "I haven't asked Alice yet, so I'd appreciate it if you don't say anything."
"Dun't vorre," agreed Ed. "I von't spil' da beans."

~~~~~~

Alice was cleaning up at the wash-stand. "I told Dolly to keep her tail to herself. I guess she thinks I'm a big horsefly. She almost knocked me off my milk stool!"
"Kin't blam' her, dose flies bit' hardt."
"Well look at my dress. It will have to go in the wash."
Tobia reported, "Vhen I go git taters, I se' Ed and Palmer in truck. Kream kins in bak."

The mention of Palmer's name made Alice's heart flutter. "I didn't even realize Palmer was here. He probably can't work in the field with all that rain last night."
"Storm skairt me, 'most yump out of bed!"
"Me too," said Alice peeking in the pot on the stove. "The ham bone is starting to smell really good."
"Ye chanj' dres', I start pelin' taters."
Alice raced upstairs and put on her brown dress with the tiny white daises. She looked in the mirror, "He loves me, he loves me not. He loves me, maybe?" After all, he had called her his daisy in the wheat field. The flame of hope was starting to burn brightly.

~~~~~~

Palmer and Ed pulled up in front of Dr. Allison's office. The black Ford C-cab sat out front with a 4-Sale-sign on the windshield. Ed was hopeful he could make a deal. Just then, Doc came roaring in with his 1921 Stutz Bearcat. It was dark green with burgundy fenders and hood. It was trimmed with brass around the front radiator and headlights. The brass hood ornament also served as a radiator cap. It had a black canvas top with an oval window in back.
"Hello Doc," greeted Palmer extending his hand.
After a hearty handshake Ed exclaimed, "Dat kar is a real humdinger!"
"I reckon so," laughed Doc. "I'm still trying to get use to the steering wheel on the right side."
Palmer asked, "Is it a two-seater?"
"Actually, it's a three-seater. It's got this little outside seat on the passenger side."
"I never se' da lik' of it befor'," remarked Ed.
"It's a beauty, that's for sure," complimented Palmer.
"Ah, yes!" agreed Doc, "but not very practical."
Ed asked, "Doc, vhat aur ye askin' fer da truck?"
"It's got a lot of country miles on it. I offered it to Rachel, but she's not ready to give up her horse. I'd like to get $300.00."
"I goin' ov'r to da bank to git da mone' rit now," announced Ed.
Doc asked, "Don't you want to drive it first Ed?"
"Nei, I 'no' ye tak' goodt care of it. I be rit back vith da kash."

~~~~~~

Ed and Palmer stepped into the kitchen.
"It sure smells good in here," replied Palmer.
Alice was taking the bread out of the oven. "We made Komla."
Ed grabbed Tobia and laid a big smack on her lips. *"Kiss da kuk, she's Norwegian,"* he sang as he swung Tobia around and around.
"Uffda! Such foolishness!" cried Tobia.
" Ve need to prakes our steps fer da next barn-razen dance," chuckled Ed. "Let's eat and after din'er ve al' goin' fishin'!"

~~~~~~

Palmer led the way through the woods to his favorite fishing spot. Tobia sat on the fishing stump and Ed fished from a large rock.
Palmer took Alice's hand, "I have a surprise for you!" He led her back to his thinking log. He had carved two entwining hearts, one with a P and the other heart with an A. "Our initials spell PA."
"That they do," giggled Alice. "This is a very pleasant surprise!"
"Would you please share my thinking log with me?" pleaded Palmer.
"I'd love too! I just want to sit here and reflect on you and all that's good."
Palmer sat down next to Alice, searching for the right words to express what was in his heart.
Alice broke the silence. "Palmer, do you believe in love at first sight?"
"I do now. The first time we met I was completely intoxicated with your big brown eyes. In a moment you had captured my heart and I would have followed you anywhere."
"Did you notice I was making cow-eyes at you?" queried Alice.
"I was too captivated by your charm to notice," confessed Palmer.
"Your sky-blue eyes held me captive. My butterflies were doing tailspins. I was in a state of unspeakable bliss."
"Alice, do you know, you are wearing my favorite dress?"
"Do you like daisies?"
"Just this one," said Palmer tenderly as he lifted Alice hand and gently kissed it.
"When I saw you coming across the wheat field in that dress, I knew at that very moment that I had met the love of my life. I think about you, us, our life together every minute of the day and night. Alice, I want to be partners for life in a bond that will last as long as life itself." Palmer reached into his pocket and took out a gold band. "Alice, I would be honored if you would be my bride."

"Yes, nothing could make me happier to spend the rest of my days loving you," came Alice's sweet reply.

Palmer slipped the gold ring on her finger. "Miss Alice, may I steal a kiss?"

"I thought you'd never ask," giggled Alice.

Palmer drew Alice into his arms and kissed her tenderly. Alice felt like her heart was flying on wings of its own. She hoped Palmer felt the same way.

"Palmer, you are so deserving of a good wife. I promise I will do my best to be a capable wife like the one in the book of Proverbs. I want to be all of that for you."

"Alice, I want to be the husband who rises each morning to praise his little daisy in the wheat field. So when do you want to get married?" Palmer didn't wait for a response. "How about tomorrow? I don't want to waste another day of my life without you."

Alice's enchanted laughter rang through the woods, "Hazel wants to be our bridesmaid. I need a few hours to sew her dress."

The Love Bug had finally caught Palmer and Alice for there is no place to hide from true love.

Chapter 17   The Rope

The smell of damp earth lingered after the soaking rainstorm. The fields were so saturated it would take another day or two before the men could get back to work. Palmer knew his father John could use an extra hand at his Blacksmith Shop. Palmer pulled Pepper's head down toward his face. "You're a good ol' boy," he crooned and rubbed behind the horse's ears. Pepper nuzzled Palmer's shoulder with his soft velvet nose and then shook his head. Palmer grabbed the bridle off the barn wall. Pepper nickered and stamped his foot impatiently. "You're anxious to get goin', aren't you boy?"
At the end of Palmer's lane, Pepper tossed his head and pricked his ears up. "I hear it too, ol' boy. The breeze seems to be playing a tune today. I know it's crazy, but it sounds like a fiddle."

~~~~~~

"Look who the cat drug in," teased Eli when Palmer walked through the door. Gunvor Torgeson and his son, Ole followed.
"Haloo!" roared Gunvor. "John da manure spreader brok' down ag'in. It's plumb worn out, 'bout rede fer da scrap pile."
"Was it full of manure this time?" asked Eli.
"Of cours' it vas, piled sky high," growled Gunvor.
John laughed, "If this keeps up, you'll soon have a new spreader. We've rebuilt most of the parts."
"Pa, you load it too heavy," advised Ole.
"I 'spect dat's true," agreed Gunvor. "Palmer, ye da man I vas hopin' to run into. I 'no' ye aur buse, but vas wonderin' if ye kin help vith hayin'? Herd's growin' so ve plant mor' alfalfa dis year. Too much fer Ole an' me to handl'."
"Let me know when you're ready."
"Ja, I vill giv' ye a holler vhen ve git it cut an' raked. Hey, Palmer, vhat's dis I hear 'bout ye git'in' married?"
"Wow, news travels like lightning around here! Who told you?"
"Ole vent over to da Hoverstens to ask Ed if he kud court his doter. Ed say Alice engag' to ye. I dink ye git a goodt von. Yes, sirree!"
"I'm always a dollar short and a day to late," complained Ole.
"Yoo-hoo!" cackled Gyda Yawnson. "Hello, men! You know there oughta be a law against men as good lookin' as you all are. My, my, Ole you sure have grown up

into a handsome lad. I know some single young ladies if you are looking for a bride." Gyda looked at Palmer and babbled on, "I personally feel that you young men would be better off with an older more experienced woman. Those young girls are so flighty, foolish too. They just don't know what they want, but an older woman like me knows exactly what she wants. Palmer, you know that Alice girl and your sister owe me an apology. I almost jumped out of my skin when they blasted the Klaxon on your new truck. How rude!"

Eli could not contain his laughter any longer and hid behind a draft horse.

"I tell you, I gave those foolish girls a good tongue-lashing! They were giggling and thought it was all fun and games. Now that's the perfect example of the difference between a girl and a woman. Those young girls are still learning the ropes around here, but a real woman already knows how to throw a lasso."

Eli stepped out from his hiding place and interrupted, "Ms. Yawnson, we've got a lot of work to do around here and it does not include chitchat!"

"Oh, I didn't come to chat. I'm handing out these flyers. Mr. Ellwood's horse barn was struck by lightning during that horrendous storm. There's going to be a barn raising and a dance. They're looking for fiddlers. Do any of you play?"

"Jake Anderson plays," reported Palmer.

"Well yes, I've already talked to Jake. He is a very talented musician. I just love his dark hair streaked with that silvery gray. He looks so distinguished, don't you think?"

"I think his wife would agree with you," spouted Eli.

"It's not easy to find any talent in this country bumpkin town," complained Gyda. "By the way, do any of you dance?"

Eli blurted, "We only go for the food!"

"Well that's okay, because I just want you all to know, I'm available if anyone needs dance lessons. I'll have you kicking up your heels in no time flat. And Eli there will be plenty of food, too. I'm bringing my prize-winning cherry pie!"

Eli piped up, "Is it left over from the fair?"

"Of course not," snapped Gyda. "Well, I'll be on my way until next time. So long! To-da-lu!"

"Let me get the door for you," offered Eli.

"Well thank you, Eli. With a little more polishing, I'll make a gentleman out of you after all."

Eli exploded after he slammed the door. "I was about ready to shove a bridle in her big mouth!"

Gunvor chuckled,"Dat voman could talk da tails right off mi Holsteins."

"I wish she would find a new man to occupy her time," stated John.

"Gyda just gave me an idea," informed Palmer.

"You mean she's good for something," sneered Eli.

"Ja, she was talkin' about ropes and a lasso. Then it struck me. Oscar likes to tie people up, right?" returned Palmer.

Eli agreed, "Ja, I'd like to put a lasso around that knothead's neck."

"That's it!" announced Palmer. "When he comes out of the tavern drunk, we'll tie him to a tree in the park until he sobers up."

"Brilliant idea!" exclaimed John. "I've got no respect for a man who beats on women and children."

"You know how much Oscar loves dogs," smirked Palmer. "We'll tie him to that tree where all the dogs in town relieve themselves."

"The doggy outhouse tree, that's a perfect spot for a drunk," laughed Ole.

Gunvor chuckled, "Now ve can't hav' people walkin' 'round Thompson drunk as a skunk and disturbin' da peace, now can ve?"

"I'll fill Oscar's pockets with cookies so he'll have something to share with his new doggy friends," snickered Eli. "Looks like Oscar will be Thompson's new dog-catcher!"

"C'mon, let's go talk to Sheriff Kirke right now," grinned Palmer. "I think the sheriff might just want to donate a big juicy steak to put in the front of Oscar's drawers."

"Ja, Oscar's doggy friends will have him naked as a plucked prairie chicken in no time flat," smirked Eli.

Chapter 18   Dance Lessons

"Eli do you know how to dance?" asked Palmer.
"Are you joshin' me? I"d rather shovel horse manure all day long then learn to dance."
"Remember when you asked me for advice about courtin' Rachel?"
"Ja, you got any ideas?"
"I sure do. You Eli Olafsen are going to learn to dance."
"Me! You got the wrong fellow. No, no, no! Out of the question!"
"Eli what are you going to do when all the young men are dancing with beautiful Rachel?"
"Aw-w-w, fiddlesticks! I'm goin' to sit in the corner and bawl my eyes out."
"Wouldn't it be better to be the fellow dancing with Rachel? Holding her soft hand and looking into those big amber eyes."
"You're killin' me, Palmer! You sure do know how to torture a guy. You're askin' too much. You know I can't stand Gyda Yawnson!"
"Oh, no, we're not going to stoop that low. I asked my sister Hazel to teach us how to dance."
"Is that the sister that's a walking encyclopedia?"
"Ja, that's Hazel. Our first lesson starts tonight."

~~~~~~

Hazel chalked four twenty-four inch squares on the grass. She added a fifth box in front of the squares for herself. She had read over the dance instructions for waltzing five more times. Hazel had practiced all day and had convinced her sisters, Mabel and Myrtle to lend a helping hand. She had set up her Duplex phonograph on the porch. Now she was ready for her dance pupils. She looked at Palmer and Eli sitting on the porch steps. *Oh, my, this is going to be a challenging assignment.*
"Okay students, everyone step into your square, with both feet together in the upper left-hand corner. Just watch me and follow. 1st bar of music—as you count 1, step back with your left foot to the lower left-hand corner. As you count 2, step diagonally with the right foot to the other back corner. Count 3—close the left foot to the right." Hazel looked over her shoulder. "Good you boys are doing great!"
"Sure we are," mumbled Eli.

"2nd bar of music—count 1 again and step forward with your right foot to the upper right corner. Count 2, step diagonally forward with your left foot to the upper left. As you count 3, close your right foot to your left. That brings us back to where we started. We'll call this corner home."
"Are we playing baseball?" asked Palmer. "1,2,3, I think, I already struck out."
"This is so fun," remarked Myrtle.
"I think your definition of fun differs greatly from mine," protested Eli.
"Now, I want everyone to practice. Repeat with the count until your feet move instinctively. Step, step, close; step, step, close; you are all doing it. See it's not that hard."
"How are you doing over there, Eli?" asked Palmer.
"I'm glad to report; I haven't stepped on myself yet."
"Is everyone ready to add the music, now?" queried Hazel.
"Hazel, do you really think a big ol' ox like me can actually learn to dance?"
"Of course you can Eli!" encouraged Hazel. "We'll have you waltzing across the barn floor in no time!"
"I can answer Eli's question with one word," laughed Palmer. "The word is Rachel!"
"Okay, I'm going to do this or die trying," hollered Eli. "Hazel get that music goin'. I can't hold these dancing feet still any longer!"
Everyone roared with laughter!
"That's the spirit Eli!" shouted Hazel as she leaped onto the porch to crank up the Duplex phonograph. "This tune is called, 'The Blue Skirt Waltz.' I'll request it for the first song at the dance, so you'll feel right at home." Hazel paused and turned back to her students. "There's one thing I forgot to tell you. In the waltz the 1st step is accented by holding it. It borrows nearly a quarter of a count from the next beat."
Palmer queried, "Is it really going to matter if we are off a quarter?"
"You'll mess up the rhythm; timing makes all the difference in the world you know."
"Listen to your teacher Palmer," smirked Eli.
Hazel played the music over and over.
"I think you have all mastered the waltz rhythm. Now we need to add a partner. Mabel you join Palmer in his square and Myrtle you dance with Eli."
"I might step on her foot and crush it," yelped Eli.

"No you won't. Let me show you," reassured Hazel. "Give me your left hand. Now put your right hand on my waist. My left hand rests on your shoulder. Myrtle get ready to turn the music on."

"Are we goin' to dance in this little square," asked Eli.

"Yes, it's all the space we need. Eli I'll step forward on my right, you'll go back on your left. I'll step back on my left; you'll step forward on your right."

"Miss Hazel, I'm sweatin' bullets!"

"You'll be fine. Myrtle, ready for the music~~~step, step, close; step, step, close; step, step, close; "Hazel and Eli moved around and around the dance square. A round of applause came from all the dance students!

"Okay, Myrtle change places with me. I'm going to count this time. We have to get the timing right. Remember the 1st step is 1 and a quarter, so hold it a second longer. Here we go, 1+, 1-2, 1-2-3, 1, 1-2, 1-2-3. Let me hear you count and remember to add the quarter on the 1st step."

1+, 1-2, 1-2-3, 1, 1-2, 1-2-3~~~ The students waltzed around and around the squares.

"You've got the Waltz rhythm," applauded Hazel. "All you need now is practice and one of these," insisted Hazel holding up Martha's mop. She had painted a girly face on the mop and added braids. "Listen up, tomorrow night we're going to learn the Waltz turn and the pursuit. Be here at 7:00 sharp!"

"Yes, ma'am!" returned Palmer.

"And try to hunt up more couples for the Virginia Reel. We'll need 6 couples or 12 people."

"Yes Teacher! Can't we use our mop dolls for partners?" quipped Palmer.

"Very funny! You better watch it Palmer. I'll put you in your dance square wearing the dunce hat."

Chapter 19   Wedding Plans

After Palmer dropped off Eli, he drove through Thompson to see if Oscar was at the tavern. Sure enough, there stood is old mule Jack tied to the hitching post. *Some people always have to learn the hard way. Oscar is one of those. He will never graduate from the School of Hard Knocks!* Palmer heaved a sigh of relief, at least Sadie and the children would be safe tonight. And he knew where to find Oscar if he was fit for work in the morning. Sheriff Kirke would have Oscar tied to his doggy tree. *What goes around comes around, "you reap what you sow." Would Oscar ever learn that too much "wine bites like a serpent?"* The threshing crew had been pushing Oscar hard and fast! Palmer had never known anyone who could whine as much as Oscar. Palmer sped over the muddy dirt roads on his way to the Hoverstens. He wanted to talk to Alice and his phone might as well be out of order with Gyda and Bertina living on the line.
Tobia met Palmer at the door, "C'mon in, ye hav' supper yet?"
"Nei, I'm too anxious to see Alice."
Tobia pushed him into a kitchen chair and started to scold, "ye vay too thin, Mr. Helgren. Ye eat now! I mak' ye moder's Swedish dish today." Tobia went to the stove and dished up a heaping plate full and set it in front of Palmer. "Ye eat," she ordered, "I get Alice."
Alice appeared in the doorway with a memo pad and a pencil. "I'm so glad you came. We need to discuss wedding plans." Alice looked at Palmer's plate heaped with noodles and meatballs. "Is mother force-feeding you again?"
"Ja, but I love all this female attention. This is delicious and I'm starving!"
Tobia set down a big glass of milk and a slice of Alice's sourdough bread smothered in butter and blackberry jam. She was wearing a grin on her face as big as Texas.
"Tobia, this is so good. Mange takk!" praised Palmer.
"Ye velkommen! I gonna fattin' ye up a lit'l."
"And I'm going to cooperate fully," grinned Palmer.
Alice was glowing with excitement as she sat down next to Palmer. "Martin and Jennie offered their home for our wedding. It's a huge, beautiful house and Jennie will have it decorated like a palace and she's going to cover her flower beds to protect them from the frost and the wedding will be on a Monday afternoon on October 30th, followed by a wedding dinner served at five o'clock. How does that sound?"
"It sounds perfect," agreed Palmer.

"What's your favorite color Palmer?"

"I don't think I have one, but I've had my eye on a navy blue suit at Erickson's Store."

"Perfect, I love navy, too. Jennie is going to decorate with pink and white. I think those colors look really nice with navy."

"So do you want Walter and I to wear white shirts?"

"Yes and I'm going to order some silk in a navy and white print to make your ties."

"Thanks that would be very special!"

"Now, for Hazel's dress, what color?"

"Let's stick with navy. You can trim it in pink."

"Palmer, I love that idea!"

"I kin do folkloric embroidery in pink," offered Tobia.

"Oh, Mother that sounds beautiful," chimed Alice. "Oh, I almost forgot the invitations. How many should we order?"

"I better get help from Mother with that," returned Palmer. "Oh, and Mother said she would like to make our wedding cake and also help with the wedding feast."

"Mange takk, helpin' hands velkommen. Palmer do ye vant a piece of pe'ch pie?"

"Tobia, if I eat another morsel my eyeballs might pop out!"

"I fix it to go, so ye kin hav' at bedtim' vith a big glas' of milk."

"Mange takk, Tobia! I know it will be delicious."

"I fattin' ye up lik' a but'er bal'!"

"Bring it on," laughed Palmer. "Alice, Hazel is teaching dance lessons. She needs 12 people or 6 couples to teach the 'Virginia Reel.' I was wondering if you would like to be my partner."

"Of course, that sounds so fun!"

"Do you know anyone else who might be interested?"

"I'll ask Josie and Elmer. They like to dance."

"Eli and I had are first waltzing lesson tonight. We're supposed to practice with a mop doll, but I'd rather dance with you. Tomorrow evening, we learn the waltz turn and the pursuit. Would you like to join me?"

"I'd love too!" came Alice's sweet reply.

Chapter 20   The Chocolate Cake

The Vage family had set up a broom making factory in the barn. The children had helped Sadie sort the broom fibers into piles from short and coarse to long and fine.
David played the fiddle as they worked. He was a natural at it and he just couldn't seem to get enough. Sadie had never had a student so gifted as her David. Whatever tune she hummed, David was able to capture the notes and make the fiddle sing. It kept the younger children entertained and they sang and danced until they were dizzy.
"Mama, how com' Papa never comes hom' no mor'?" asked Leah.
"I'm sure I don't know," replied Sadie. But sadly she did know. Oscar had bragged about spending time at the tavern with his 'painted ladies' as he called them.
"We dun't care," added Lydia. "We hav' fun when he not here!"
"I hope he never comes back," stated David. "We can't play the fiddle when he's here!"
"He skair me," confessed little Rachel.
"Mama, tell me if I have the notes right for 'Red River Valley'."
"Okay, David let's hear it. If you get all the notes right we'll bake a chocolate cake to celebrate."
"Did you say cake? I'm gonna do it if it takes all night!"
Ruth drilled a hole at the top of each wooden handle, so the brooms could be hung up when finished. Sarah drilled two small holes at the base of the broom handles. Sadie would use the tiny holes for threading the wire that would hold the straw fibers to the handle as she wrapped them around, layer by layer. Sadie used a machine called a Winder. She had found it here in the barn over thirteen years ago when Oscar brought her here. She knew it was used for making brooms, because her grandparents had taught her the art of broom-making. Sadie and the Winder had spent much time together and she called it her old friend. Oscar had tied her to it whenever he left the farm. He had threatened to kill her if she ever tried to run away again. Those were days of dark despair and hopeless dread! Her heart still cried out with silent tears. The Winder was designed to wind wire and broomcorn around the handle. Sadie powered it by using the foot pedals. An old cast-iron chain turned the spindle. The Winder's bearings were made of wood. Sadie thought the machine still worked remarkably well considering its age. Sadie adjusted the tension on the wire as she added each layer. The fibers had to be wrapped tight enough to stay in place for the life of the broom.

~~~~~~

Sheriff Kirke dismounted from his horse and peered through the sagging screen door. The old log cabin was clean as a whistle, but lifeless. It appeared that no one was home, but music from a fiddle was coming from the barn. And the most beautiful voice that Michael had ever heard was singing, 'The Red River Valley'.

~~~~~~

Sadie looked up from her work at the Winder. There stood a tall, well-built man with handsome features, honey-colored hair, bright blue eyes, a friendly smile and a cowboy hat in his hand.
"Ma'am, I'm sorry if I startled you. My name is Michael Kirke. I'm the sheriff for King township."
Sadie rose on trembling legs and extended her thin, work-worn hand. Michael gently clasped it in his. He stared into her emerald green eyes. They were like two glistening jewels, but in those beautiful eyes fear lurked.
"Please, don't be frightened," he said with a soft, sympathetic voice. Michael saw a smile starting to creep across her pale, weary face. She was a beautiful woman with a face as delicate as a flower. Her golden hair was tied back with a piece of twine. He could tell her muscular arms were accustomed to strenuous labor.
"It's nice to meet you. I'm Sadie Vage and these are my children."
Sarah had seated all the children on the floor where they sat quietly. David was carefully putting the fiddle back in its case.
"They are all as beautiful as their mother," remarked Michael. "You must be very proud!"
"Thank you, I am," blushed Sadie.
"And you young man are a very talented fiddle player!" said Michael smiling at David.
"Thank you, very much, sir," said David proudly.
"How old are you son?"
"I'm eight years old, sir."
"His name David," piped up little Rachel.
"Well thank you for telling me that. Names are a very important thing to know. Now let me guess, I bet your name is-s-s, ah-h, Sugar."
"Nei, it not Shuger."

"Now don't tell me, it's right here on the tip of my tongue. Ah-h-h, you look mighty sweet. I bet they call you, Sweet Pea."
Little Rachel shook her head.
"Did I get it wrong again? Okay, can I have just one more try?"
Rachel nodded her little head.
"I know I'm sure I've got it this time. It's, it's, it's…my Darlin' Clementine!"
Giggles erupted from all the children!
"Me Rachel!"
"Oh, my, that's an absolutely beautiful name! I'm so glad your mother named you instead of me." Michael looked at David, "Who taught you to play that fiddle young man?"
"Mama did sir," answered David beaming with pride.
"Call me Michael, well your mother is an excellent teacher."
"Do you play, Michael?" asked David.
"I play piano. My mother was the piano teacher, so I didn't have a choice." Michael mimicked his mother, *"Michael where do you think you are going?"*
"Outside to play ball Mother. *"Oh no you are not!"* "But Mother Timmy's coming over to play catch." *"Michael, the only thing that you are going to play is piano!"* "But Mother Timmy's waiting for me." *"Sit down and start playing 'Swan Lake.'"* "How about 'Chopsticks?'" *"Michael, do I have to glue you to the piano bench? Start playing, 'Swan Lake.' You will thank me for this someday. When you get all the notes right you may go play ball."* Well, I really liked playing ball, so I learned to play the piano, too. And Mother was right as mothers always are. I'm glad I learned to play, both baseball and piano." Michael turned to speak to Sadie. "Mrs. Vage, I wanted to ride out here and tell you your husband is okay. He's been tied up lately. I hear he has a mean streak when he's drinking and I don't want him to hurt you or the children. So when he comes out of the tavern drunk, I tie him to a tree until he sobers up."
"Thank you, Mr. Kirke!" exclaimed Sadie.
Michael could see relief written all over Sadie's face. All the children applauded at the good news.
"Well, the thanks go to Palmer Helgren. He came up with the brilliant idea."
"Palmer aur friend," spouted little Rachel.
"Well, I'd like to be your friend, too. So don't forget my name. My name is-s-s, ah-h-h, my name is-s, oh, goodness, I forgot my name, again. Oh, dear, what is my name?"
Sadie's children were busting at the seams with laughter!

Little Rachel spoke up, "It's ok, I help you. Michael is your name."
"Oh, thank you, Rachel. A fellow needs to know who he is. Mrs. Vage, no one needs to know that I was here today." Michael saw another wave of relief sweep over Sadie's face.
"Is it a secret?" asked David.
"It sure is," said Michael zipping his lips closed with two fingers.
The children mimicked Michael with imaginary zippers.
 They watched as he crossed the yard singing, *"From this valley they say you are leaving. We shall miss your bright eyes and sweet smile. For you take with you all of the sunshine. That has brightened our pathway a while."* Michael mounted his horse, waved, tipped his cowboy hat and disappeared down the lane singing, *"Then come sit by my side if you love me. Do not hasten to bid me adieu. Just remember the Red River Valley and the cowboy that's loved you so true..."*
"We need to be more careful children," sighed Sadie.
"That's for sure," replied Sarah.
"I'll hide the fiddle. Don't worry Mama, he won't tell." Then David planted a big kiss on his mother's worried face.
Sadie hung another unfinished broom on the barn wall. She would flatten the brooms by stitching them with colored twine. It was done by hand using a double-pointed needle that she pushed back and forth through the fibers. It was her evening job, but it would have to wait. Sadie owed David a chocolate cake.

Chapter 21   No Stone Unturned

As Michael Kirke rode back to town he thought about all the books he'd read as a boy. He loved mystery and detective books. He had always tried to solve the case before he reached the last chapter. The more he mulled things over in his mind the more they just did not add up.

Sadie is a young, beautiful woman. She could turn every head in town. So, why would she marry Oscar Vage? Not that Oscar looks bad, but he is old enough to be Sadie's father. Oscar is getting bald on top, beer belly, cranky, lazy, a drunkard, and not very good husband material. Was it an arranged marriage? No that definitely does not make sense. Oscar is not wealthy by a long shot! Could Sadie be a mail-order-bride? If that was the case, Sadie would have run like the dickens when she met Oscar! David said he is 8, but he has two older sisters. So the oldest must be about 11 or 12. Say, Sadie was 18 when her first child was born. Then she'd be 30 now. No way, Sadie could pass for one of the children. I've been sheriff for almost 5 years, so why have I never seen Sadie and the children in town? Why aren't the children enrolled in school?

It was time to put his detective skills to the test.

Oscar works for Palmer. I wonder what he knows. Rachel Allison must have delivered some of those children. Maybe she can give me a lead.

There was something downright fishy about this case and Michael was determined to get to the bottom of it!

~~~~~~

Palmer and Rachel met Sheriff Kirke at his office.

"Palmer tell me what you know about Oscar Vage."

"He's lazy, eats, drinks and lies too much. He treats his mules better than his wife. He claims he traded one of his best mules for Sadie. She's his property and he'll do what he pleases with her."

"Oscar sounds like a real tyrant! And what kind of a father trades his daughter for a mule?"

"Michael, I asked Oscar the same question. He claims her father was stone drunk."

"Palmer, when did you first meet Sadie?"

"I saw their crops were not harvested, so I went over there to see if I could help. Sadie said she needed help. Did I know a mid-wife? I asked if she needed a ride to town. She said Oscar forbid her leaving the farm. I told her I would ride into town and tell Caroline Allison."

"Rachel were you there when Sadie gave birth?"

"Yes, I was eight years old. Mother and I left as soon as Palmer told us. We barely made it on time. Sadie fell in love with baby Sarah immediately, but she said Oscar would be upset, because he wanted sons to work the farm. When mother asked Sadie for her age, she didn't know. Sadie said that was one of the many things she had forgotten. She told us that she had suffered from severe headaches and was trying so hard to remember who she was and how she got here. Mother examined Sadie's head and found a scar under her hair, but Sadie didn't remember hitting her head. She said all she knew was what Oscar had told her. Oscar claimed that he had traded her for his best mule when her father was drunk. He told her that her name was Sadie and she said that sounded familiar. Oscar claimed the preacher had come to the house to marry them, because Sadie was sick in bed. Sadie couldn't remember any of it. Sadie asked us where she was. When Mother told her, Thompson, Iowa, Sadie said she had never heard of it. Sadie told us that sometimes she had flashbacks of the past and some things were coming back. Music was still in her head and she remembered songs, Bible accounts and scriptures she had memorized. She was so grateful for those memories because it helped her deal with her depression. When Mother told Father about Sadie he said she probably had suffered from a severe head concussion and had a form of amnesia. It is usually caused by a blow to the head. Sadie always has a lot of bruises especially around her wrists and ankles. Recently, David told me that Oscar ties her to the bedpost. I so wish Mother was here; I know she would remember many more details."

"Thanks Rachel, you have been very helpful. Palmer how old do you think Oscar is?"

"I'm not sure Michael, I'd say close to fifty."

"I keep askin' myself, why would a young beauty like Sadie marry an old man like Oscar Vage?"

"I've asked myself the same question many times," remarked Palmer. "I have a feeling Sadie did not have a choice."

"Michael, I'm so glad you are looking into this. I've prayed for years that Sadie's full memory will be restored and this unsolved mystery will be resolved," sighed Rachel.

"Well, things just don't add up! There's something very wrong and I'm determined to get to the bottom of this if it takes the rest of my life. I promise to leave no stone unturned. I guess I'll start at the court house. Maybe the date on that marriage license will give us a clue."

Chapter 22   My Lady and Sir Galahad

Eli took a bath scrubbing himself squeaky clean. He had to get over to the Allisons to ask Rachel to the dance. Palmer had advised him to hurry before someone else got the jump on him. He hoped he wasn't too late. He wished he could take two year old Ardis along. That little chap knew how to charm the ladies. When dance lessons were over maybe he should take charm lessons from Ardis.
Eli knocked on the Allison's front door.
Doc answered, "Good Evening Eli, what can I do for you?"
"Oh, ahh, I'm not sick."
"Well, I'm glad to hear that. You look healthy as a horse, Eli."
"Yes sir, I am. Ahh, the reason I came over here is, ahh I would like to talk to Rachel. Is she home?"
"Rachel just rode in. She's around back in the stable."
"Thanks sir, I mean Doc. Thanks Doc. Maybe I can give her a helping hand."
Doc chuckled as he closed the door. "He's as nervous as an old creeping turtle crossing a busy street."
Rachel was dressed in a brown Bolero leather jacket, matching riding skirt and boots. Eli couldn't help but notice the flattering fit. She was loosening the cinch on her saddle. Eli stepped through the door and easily lifted the saddle off the horse.
"Sneaking up on me, Eli Olafsen," teased Rachel.
"Just out rescuing maidens in distress with by Oldsmobile Runabout."
"Well, thank you Kind Sir. I love having a knight in shining armor at my side."
"My Lady, I am at your beck and call." Eli grabbed the curry-comb and started brushing down the mare. "She's a beautiful horse! What's her name?"
"I'd tell you, but I'm sure you'll laugh."
"Why would I laugh?"
"I got this horse when I was ten years old. Father said I could name her anything I wanted," explained Rachel.
"So what did you name her?" asked Eli again.
"Promise you will not laugh."
"Why would I laugh? So what did you name her?"
"Sugar Lips."
Eli tried to suppress his laughter to no avail.
"See you're laughing Eli."
"That I am! Why Sugar Lips?"

"She liked sugar cubes so much and she still does."
"Well, I think Sugar Lips is a very S-W-E-E-T name."
"There you go laughing again!"
"My Lady, I'm doing my best to stomp down my laughter," snickered Eli.
"Of course, you are," smiled Rachel. "I'll have to forgive you this time. After all, laughter is cheap medicine."
Eli stared at Rachel. The declining sunlight coming through the west window highlighted her glowing mahogany hair. Their eyes met.
"My Lady, your lustrous amber eyes hold me captive. I need rescuing."
Now Rachel was the one laughing. "Sir, how shall I rescue you?"
"My Lady, come to the dance with me Saturday night."
"Sir Galahad, I would be honored to dance with such a handsome knight."

Chapter 23   The Dance

The talk in Thompson was buzzing like an over-active bee hive. The news of the coming barn-raising and dance spread far and wide. Karina Anderson, Thompson's telephone operator hadn't had a break in weeks. Erickson's General Store was sold out of men's blue-jeans and full-sweep skirts. Their fabric stash had never been so low. Shorty, the town's cobbler was sold out of boots and stayed up until wee hours of the night working on new orders. The Willow Creek Lumberyard was delivering building supplies to Mr. Ellwood's farm. The men sharpened their tools and the women swapped recipes and planned meals. Hazel's dance students practiced their steps every spare minute they could find. They were doing do-si-dos and promenades in their dreams. Mr. Ellwood poured the concrete floor and stacked the lumber near the job site. Tables and benches were set up for the food. Everything was ready for the big event.

The men started on the horse stable early Saturday morning. The barn went up quickly. By noon all the framing was finished. After the noon meal the men swarmed the roof like carpenter ants. The ring of hammers driving down nails could be heard a mile away. The barn was finished by four o'clock and the men hurried home to do chores and get cleaned up for the dance.

Eli had practiced his dance steps so much he was afraid he'd worn his boots out. But a little grease had spruced them up. He wore the navy and white striped shirt that Alice had made with a new pair of blue-jeans.

Palmer took a bath and put on his new blue-plaid shirt made by his bride-to-be. He pulled on his new pair of blue-jeans. He had even bought a new belt for the event. Palmer had polished his boots until they shone. He looked in the looking glass. If only he could get this unruly wavy hair under control. Eli would be here any minute.

Eli and Palmer pulled up to the Hoversten's porch. Palmer met Alice coming down the steps. She looked lovely in her blue calico full-circle skirt. Her blue blouse was trimmed with matching calico around the bib yoke and sleeves.

The Oldsmobile Runabout headed for Rachel's house.

Eli felt like his heart would jump right out of his chest. Rachel stood on the porch wearing a waltz length full skirt of navy blue satine. Her white blouse was trimmed with matching blue piping.

Eli leaped up the steps by twos. Taking Rachel's arm he said softly, "Ready Sugar Lips, oh, I mean, my Lady."

"Of course, what took you so long, Sir Galahad?" teased Rachel.

When they entered the new barn they saw Mr. Ellwood talking to Jake Anderson. They both looked worried.

Palmer asked, "Is everything okay?"

Jake explained, "Thomas Livingston bailed out because of a broken wrist. He loaned us his fiddle and banjo, but we've got no one to play them. Johannes Nelson was drafted for a wedding dance in Minnesota. I'm the only fiddler left."

Mr. Ellwood spoke up next. "I hate to disappoint my neighbors. You boys worked so hard today, volunteering your time and labor to help me. I feel like I'm letting everyone down. Well, I'll drag the piano out here. Maybe we'll find someone who can play."

Rachel stepped forward, "I know someone who can play. Stall for an hour. We'll be back!" She grabbed a box under the food table. "Help me fill this up for Sadie and the children."

Eli sacked up cookies. Palmer added ham and fried chicken. Alice put in bread and biscuits. Rachel topped it off with cheese and grapes.

"We'll be right back!" exclaimed Rachel.

Eli and Rachel heard music coming from the barn. Someone was playing, "The Blue Skirt Waltz."

Sadie and the children were surprised and excited to see them. But not as surprised as Eli and Rachel, for the player of the fiddle was young David.

Rachel explained their dilemma.

Sadie wondered what she should do. *It was a huge risk! A dangerous risk! Was it worth the cost?*

Eli spoke up, "Sheriff Kirke said he would make sure Oscar's tied up tonight."

"But someone will surely spill the beans," protested Sadie.

"I thought of that," remarked Rachel. "No one knows you and we can say you wish to remain anonymous."

"Please Mama, we've never been to town," begged Sarah.

"I can play the fiddle," offered David.

Was it worth the risk? Ja, it was! "Children put on your very best clothes. We are going to a dance!"

Rachel helped dress the little ones.

Eli washed faces and hands. "Now ya'll stay clean!"
Sadie put on a dress and shoes she had found in Rachel's share bag.
"I've got the fiddle," hollered David as they all piled into Eli's car.
The children were ecstatic with excitement. The first time off the farm and the first time they had ever eaten so well. They squealed with delight when they tasted the grapes!

~~~~~~

The barn was full of people eating, laughing, talking, but what they really wanted was music.
Sadie was so nervous! Could she play after all these years? Her mind drifted back to her childhood. Her family was known for their entertainment at weddings and barn-raisings. People called them the Music-Makers. *I can do this, I think.* Jake told her to start and he and David would follow with the fiddles. Sadie sat down at the piano. She took a deep breath. Music had always brought her boundless joy. She needed to share that joy with this crowd tonight. The thought of bringing happiness to her neighbors gave her the needed courage. Sadie struck the keys and she sang, *"Roll out the barrel, we'll have a barrel of fun, roll out the barrel, we'll have the blues on the run..."* Sadie had the crowd's attention. They were clapping, singing and stomping their feet. Jake and David had followed with the fiddles as promised. Sadie was proud to have a part in filling every corner of this new barn with music tonight. When the applause died down, she played, "Hot Time in the Old Town," "Buffalo Gals Come Out to Nite," "Turkey in the Straw," and "Little Brown Jug." When she looked up she saw Eli and Palmer dragging Sheriff Kirke to the piano.
"Like always, I've been drafted again," laughed Michael.
"I'm glad you decided to join us," smiled Sadie.
Jake handed Sadie a fiddle. Now she really felt at home. The fiddle was her first love!
Jake announced, "next: 'The Blue Skirt Waltz!'"
Tobia and Martha volunteered to watch Sadie's children.
Palmer took Alice's hand and walked toward the dance floor. They hoped they would make Hazel proud.
"Those two are just glowing with love for each other," remarked Martha.
"Love is sort of leaking out all over this place tonight," laughed John.
"Ja, plac' kud be flood'd bi midnite," chuckled Ed.

Eli took Rachel's hand. *Palmer was right; here I am holding the girl of my dreams in my arms tonight.* Rachel was a spirited dancer, but Eli's long legs kept up with her stride.

Skirts swirled gracefully as couples whirled across the floor. Their rhythmic movements looked like children chasing fireflies.

Sadie looked down at David. Her eight year old son was having the time of his life. The fiddlers played, "Tucker Waltz," "The Blue Danube," "The Happy Wanderer," and "You Can't Be True."

"Anyone ready for square dancing?" asked Jake.

Cheers went up from the crowd!

"I need six couples for the 'Virginia Reel,' line up!"

Sadie led with the tune of "Irish Washerwomen."

Jake's voice rang out with the Patter Call! **"Forward and bow to your partners all. Right hand 'round, around the hall. Left hand back and don't be slack. Two hands round and around you go. And now your partners do-si-do..."**

The fiddlers played, "Golden Slippers," "Camptown Races," and "Darling Nellie Gray."

Jake announced, "Sorry folks, Michael and I are all tuckered out. But heads up, we've got entertainment from the next generation. We'll be right back after we check out that keg of root beer donated by Johnson's Drugstore."

Michael asked Jake, "Have you ever seen anyone so talented?"

Jake answered, "I won't be surprised when David wins the State Fiddlers Competition someday."

"His toughest competitor will be his mother," laughed Michael.

Rachel helped Sadie line up the children. They sang, "Pop Goes the Weasel." The twins Joel and Jonathan exchanged wide-eyed looks and then popped up late as always. The next tune was "Oh Susannah." Sadie accompanied them with the banjo. *"I come from Alabama with the banjo on my knee; I'm going to Louisiana, my true love for to see..."*

The crowd shouted, **"Encore! Encore!"**

The children knew what that meant this time. The children sang, "Shoo Fly," "Bingo," "Home on the Range," "Shall Be Comin' Around the Mountain," and the "Wells Fargo Wagon."

Then David sang a Missouri Folk Song called "Great Grand-Dad."

David played the fiddle as Michael sang, "Red River Valley."

To end the evening, Sadie accepted requests from the crowd. Sadie's beautiful melodious voice climbed to the rafters of the new barn on that memorable night.

Chapter 24   Halley's Comet

Talk of the dance lingered for weeks afterwards. Gyda Yawnson and Bertina Fardal spend hours questioning the residents of Thompson. They claimed they wouldn't have a day's rest until they found out who the mystery performers were. The problem was no one seemed to know.

~~~~~~

Palmer worked long hours bringing in the harvest. He wanted to be finished before the wedding. He had planned a two week Honeymoon trip to Duluth, Minnesota. He had reserved a boat and a cabin on the lake. Palmer missed Alice so much he could hardly bear it. So he borrowed Hazel's phonograph and on Saturday nights they used his empty dining room for a dance hall.
"You women have out done yourselves again," complimented Walter. "The meal was delicious!"
"Finger-licken' good," added Palmer.
"Would you like a slice of cherry pie," asked Mary.
Alice added, "There are also cinnamon rolls."
"I'll be too full for dancin' if I eat another morsel," said Eli.
"It's a beautiful evening. Let's sit outside and enjoy the harvest moon and stars tonight," suggested Rachel.
"I might get bit by a skeeter!" exclaimed Eli.
"So the mighty knight is afraid of a little mosquito bite," teased Rachel. "I promise to kiss it and make it all better."
Eli sprang up from the table and started for the door," I'm goin' skeeter hunting!"
Laughter filled Palmer's kitchen. After the dishes were done everyone headed for Palmer's front porch.
"Does anyone remember Halley's comet in 1910?" asked Palmer.
"Who could forget that?" remarked Walter.
"I remember how cold it was," stated Mary. "It was January, so we all bundled up in our winter coats and ran outside."
"I think I was only six, but I remember it well," said Alice. "I gazed in awe at that glittering display in the sky!"
Eli added, "I remember the head of the comet was an orange-yellow color trailed by a milky-white tail. It really stood out against that dark purple sky."

Rachel smiled, "I remember telling Father that the star had shining white hair streaming out from it and I wanted hair just like that."
Palmer stated, "They say Halley's comet will return in 76 years. We won't see it again, but our grandchildren might."
"Have you ever gazed at the stars and wondered where they end?" asked Eli.
Palmer answered, "Ja, but only their Creator knows. Like a vast army, their Commander orders their movements. Only he knows their where-abouts. When I stare into the vastness of space, I feel like I get a tiny glimpse into the limitless mind of the Commander of the Stars."

~~~~~~

Sadie and the children had finished the evening chores.
"What we havin' for supper?" asked David.
Sadie answered, "I made a big pan of cornbread."
Ruth reported, "We've got fresh-churned butter to go on top."
"Good, I'm starvin'!" exclaimed David.
"Me hungre too," agreed little Rachel.
"We've got five eggs left," explained Sadie. "We can save them for breakfast or scramble them to go with the cornbread."
"Better save them for breakfast," advised Sarah.
"Mama, I'll get us a pail of water from the well," volunteered David.
"Thank you David. You are always so thoughtful," praised Sadie.
"Well, I'm the man of the house now and I'm goin' to take care of you Mama."
"And a good man you are David."
David pulled his heavy load to the top of the well. When he looked up, he saw Oscar and old Jack coming up the lane. A grip of fear began to seize David and the rope slipped through his small hands. As he ran pell-mell to the house he thought about the heap of sadness and grief soon to start! "Mama! Pa is comin'!!!"
A shroud of darkness always hung over the Vage farm when Oscar was home and the bad news swept the house like a fever.
Sadie's pulse quickened and she felt rigid with fear!
David saw worry carved on his mother's blanched face. "Mama, it will be okay, I hid Pa's strap."
The ache in Sadie's scarred heart made her feel so utterly weary. She looked at her sad children. They were frozen up like icicles. "Children you must be on your

very best behavior. Sarah and Ruth please change the twin's diapers. I best get supper on the table."

Soon they heard Oscar bellowing like an enraged bull. The cross, cranky, old man had a short fuse and it was about to blow like an erupting volcano. He was whining, cuzzing, rantin' and ravin' and not a word of it made any sense!

Sadie and David sprang out the door. Oscar had fallen off old Jack, but he still held his whiskey bottle in his hand. He took a big swig and let out a loud belch.

Oscar hollered, "Boy I need ye to fetch an' tote. Git licker in haus'! Ye would larn a heap if ye'd hark to me!"

David pulled two whiskey bottles out of the saddle bag. Troubles were about to multiply!

Oscar looked terrible. His piercing eyes were blood shot and his chin whiskered. His body emitted a rank, foul smell as he swung his flailing arms.

Sadie said cautiously, "Oscar would you like me to help you down to the creek? A bath might feel good."

Oscar struggled to his feet yelling, "Wh-what? Shut ye trap! Dun't ye dar' sass me! Ye wish ye never saw da lite of day vhen I git dun vith ye! Hankerin' to thrash ye'all!"

Oscar refused to be silent when he was drunk. Sadie thought it would be easier to shut up a stone!

Oscar staggered towards the door. "Sadie if ye ain't got supper rede, I goin' to skin ye aliv'!"

The children were huddled in a corner near the old fireplace.

"Yawl hush! Scat! Git outta h-here! I aimin' to tan ye'all jist fer da fun of it!" sneered Oscar as he sat down at the table.

The children tiptoed towards the door walking softly as if the dead could be disturbed.

"Dis cornbre'd all ye got," complained Oscar. "Fry me four eggs!"

The children were outside the kitchen window listening to Oscar's bellowing.

"There goes our breakfast," whispered Sarah sadly.

"Ye keep youn'uns out! I got achin' he'd!" Oscar stopped to take another swig of whiskey. Then he started woofing down cornbread. "Rede fer mi eggs."

"Oscar the stove is out. I need to get more kindling."

"Sadie ye ain't worth ye weight in hors' manur'! I shulda pick ye sister. Maybe she 'no' how to kuk!"

~~~~~~

Sheriff Kirke rode into town and noticed Oscar's mule was gone. He ran into the tavern! "Charlie, where's Oscar?"
"He bought three bottles of whiskey. Said he's drinking at home from now on."
Michael mounted his horse, wheeled around and headed for the Vage farm.

~~~~~~

Sadie set down Oscar's fried eggs and reached for the pan of cornbread. Oscar grabbed her small wrist with an iron-like grip! "Ye ain't takin' mi cak'!"
"But the children need some supper," begged Sadie.
"Ve got too mane mouths to feed round here. No mor' sup'er fer ye an' youn'uns!"
Oscar relinquished his death grip to take another drink.
"Oscar I can teach music lessons. It will bring in more income."
"Nei, I got bet'er ide-e," said Oscar laughing heinously. "Gerls aur no account to me. Dey could turn out lik' ye! I dink Sarah 'bout ol' enof to trad' off fer a goodt hors'. She goodt lukin' gerl, it von't be hardt to git rid of her."
"Oscar, please don't do this!"
"Dun't sass me! Mind mad' up! Vhen I tak' milk kow over to Torgesons to git her bred, I gonna talk to Gunvor 'bout it! I hear Ole lukin' fer bride! I dink I can git three milk kows an' a hors'!" Then Oscar roared with his heinous laugh!
Sadie felt like throwing up. It was hard to breathe. Her vision was blinded with tears. A searing pain gripped her womb!
Oscar continued with his acid tongue. "Vhat's da mat'er Sadie? Ye luk lik' ye swal'ow a hors'. Vhat ye dink I wuz gonna do vith al' dese gerls?" Oscar roared with his evil laugh and reached for his bottle.
We have to get out of here! But how? If I take Buttercup, Oscar might have me arrested for stealing. Without the cow, I can't feed my children. Where can we go?
Another contraction rolled over Sadie and she leaned against the cook-stove.
Tears were streaming down Sarah's face. "He's going to sell me."
"Nei, he ain't," said David quietly. "We are gonna run away in the morin'."
Then they heard their mother cry out in fear! "Oscar my labor is starting! Please go get Rachel!"
"No von comes on mi properte!" roared Oscar. "Ye ought to 'no' how to birth by now!"
Sadie stumbled to the bed. *It's too early for my baby to come. I have to stop these contractions.*

"Sarah, I'm goin' for help," whispered David. "Sneak around back to the bedroom window and tell Mama. If you get caught, run like a jack rabbit and hide in the woods." David bailed onto Jack and raced down the lane.

~~~~~~

Max perked up his ears and growled. "Someone's comin'," said Palmer getting to his feet staring into the darkness.
Soon David appeared on the mule with a tearstained face. "Please help! Pa is drunk and Mama's baby is comin'! She needs Rachel!"
"Tell her I'm on my way!" exclaimed Rachel.
David wheeled Jack around and disappeared as quickly as he had come.
Eli ran to start his car. Everyone piled in. Rachel was thankful she had brought her medical bag. The Oldsmobile roared down Palmer's lane.

~~~~~~

Sadie wanted to cry out in her anguish, but with every labored breath she felt her strength ebbing away. Intense pain coursed through her exhausted body and she was too weary to keep up the fight. Like the grains of sand in an hour glass, Sadie felt her life flowing away. *If only I could remember how to pray. Mama said your name is Jehovah. Now I remember Psalm 83:18; "That men may know that thou, whose name alone is JEHOVAH, art the most high." Oh Jehovah, please hear the prayer of your lowly slave girl. I know I'm not worthy and I ask nothing for myself, but please Jehovah send someone to love my children…..*Sadie's arm fell to her side.
Michael Kirke could hear Oscar yelling as he approached the log cabin. "Sadie!!! G-git out of dat bed or I d-drag ye out by ye h-h-hair! Dis tim' I-I tie ye upsid' down! T-tan ye g-g-goodt!!!"
Sarah ran to Michael with eyes streaming of tears. "Mama needs help and Pa won't let me in!"
"Don't worry darling, I'll take care of her!" Michael almost ripped the sagging screen door off its hinges as he rushed into the cabin. He raced toward a ragged blanket hanging from the ceiling in the corner of the cabin.
Sadie lay on the bed limp as a wilted flower. Her face was pale and lifeless. Her thin white hands almost seemed transparent. *Is Sadie dead?* Michael struggled to force the thought out of his mind. He got down on his knees and gently lifted her

frail hand. "Sadie, Sadie, it's Michael Kirke, please don't give up! Hang on for your children. Please Sadie your children need you. We all do!"

Someone is calling, it sounds like Michael's voice. Don't give up, children need you!

Palmer and Eli finished off the screen door as they entered the cabin! Rachel and Alice rushed to Sadie's side. Walter and Mary comforted the frightened children.

"H-huh! G-get o-out!!!" screeched Oscar. "I-I uh g-gonna k-k-kill ye! G-g-g-e-t-t ye s-s-stinkin' h-hands-s off m-me!"

"We're goin' outside Oscar, get up!" commanded Palmer.

Oscar was simmering with rage! "I-In a p-p-pig's eye! H-hu-com' ye h-here?"

"Oscar you smell so bad you must be rotting!" exclaimed Eli.

"I-I g-gonna s-s-send ye p-p-pack-kin'! Ah,vay v-vith yawl! Yawl r-r-riffraff! D-dat's v-vhat ye aur!!!"

"Sheriff Kirke, what do we do with this weasel?" asked Palmer.

"Let's tie him to this tree."

"Y-ye c-c-can't! I-I on mi p-p-properte! Y'all in c-c-cahoots! I-I n-need d-drink!"

"We'd love to throw you in the well," stated Eli. "But I don't want to pollute good drinking water."

"Ya,Yawl g-gonna g-git it v-vith b-b-both b-b-barros!"

"Sheriff, do we have to put up with this?" asked Palmer.

"No sir! It's beyond the call of duty! I say let's gag the stinkin' weasel!"

Eli pulled a rag, a once- upon-a- time towel, off the clothesline.

Oscar growled, "G-G-r-r-r! I-I b-b-bite ye!"

"So your doggy friends taught you how to growl did they?" laughed Eli. "Dogs know how to take good care of weasels!"

Alice appeared in the doorway. "Rachel needs Doc, please hurry!"

Eli started his car and Palmer raced home! He ran to the kitchen phone and cranked the handle quickly! Karina answered, "Number please?"

"Karina, please connect me with Doc Allison and hurry!!!"

"R-i-n-g! R—i—n—g---! R-i-n-g! R-i-n-g! R—i—n—g---!"

Please be home Doc! Please pick up! C'mon Doc, please pick up!!!

"Hello!"

"Doc, this is Palmer Helgren. Rachel's at the Vage farm. She needs help, please hurry!"

"On my way!"

Palmer raced back to the Vage farm. It seemed like an eternity waiting for Doc!

"Sheriff, I need to talk to you," explained David.

"Call me Michael, son. Now, tell me your concerns."

"In the morinin' we are goin' to run away. Pa is mean! He hurts us with the strap. He ties Mama up and whips her. I'm the man of the house now and I ain't goin' to have it no more. We gotta leave here and never come back! There's an old cart behind the barn. Can you help me fix the broken wheel?"

Michael wrapped his arms around David. "Son, you are a young man way beyond your years .Don't worry, I'm going to take care of everything. But right now, I need you to go with Walter and Mary. They'll feed you supper and take care of you."

"Thank you Michael, you are a very good man!"

Walter was loading the children into his wagon.

David looked at Oscar and stated loud and clear, "you'll never whip my Mama again! And I'm takin' the fiddle with me! Wait just a minute Walter, I gotta get my fiddle!" Then David raced toward the barn!

Chapter 25   Halleujah, Amen!

Sadie opened her eyes. *Where am I?* She was in a beautiful bedroom in a comfy feather bed. *I must be dreaming!* She looked down at her pink nightgown. The front yoke was enriched with ornate embroidery. It was beautiful and so was the quilt on the bed.
Rachel opened the bedroom door with a breakfast tray. "Welcome back Sadie. You sure had us all worried!"
"Where am I?"
"You're safe Sadie and your children are fine. This is Michael Kirke's house. Have you ever had breakfast in bed?"
"Nei, never!"
"Let's sit you up, you must be starving!"
"How long have I been here?"
"Several days. We knew you'd be back because you've been talking in your sleep."
"I have."
"Yes and we believe your memory is restored completely."
"Really, oh Rachel, that would be a dream come true!" cried Sadie. "Who made this delicious breakfast?"
"Alice Hoversten did. Palmer picked a bride that sure can cook!"
"I've never tasted anything so good," agreed Sadie.
The door burst open and eight smiling faces all jabbering at the same time surrounded Sadie.
"Mama, ye woke up!" cried little Rachel.
"Alice measured us! She's going to make us coats and school clothes," explained Ruth.
Leah asked, "Can we go to school Mama?"
Lydia interrupted, "Michael said we can!"
"No, he said we have to ask you first," corrected Ruth.
"Mama, you oughta see our bedroom. We have real beds now," said Sarah proudly.
"Michael is teaching us how to play the piano," reported David. "And I'm teaching him how to play the fiddle."
Michael peeked around the door frame, "Speaking of Michael, here he is!"
The children all ran to Michael and smothered him with hugs and kisses!
"Rachel, if kisses are good medicine, I must be the healthiest man in town," laughed Michael.

"I do believe you are getting more than your share," smiled Rachel.

Alice appeared in the doorway. "Who's ready for breakfast?"

A mighty shout of happy chattering voices filled the room as the carefree children followed Alice like ducklings in a row.

"So how is the lovely mother of all those rowdy children this morning?" asked Michael.

"Just fine," blushed Sadie. "I'm a little jealous though. You stole all my kisses."

"I'm sure they saved some for their mama. They love you so much, Sadie!"

Rachel picked up the empty tray. "Michael, did you have breakfast?"

"Yes ma'am. Alice stuffed me just like a turkey and I enjoyed every bite!"

"I'm going to go downstairs and help Alice with the children," reported Rachel. "Michael, you are the new nurse-maid."

"Rachel, can you order me one of those cute little nurse hats?" laughed Michael.

"As you wish, Sheriff Kirke," smiled Rachel.

"Sadie, do you feel like talking?"

"Sure."

Michael pulled up a chair next to the bed and took Sadie's small hand in his. "Sadie, I'm so very sorry you lost your baby. It was a little boy and I named him Noah. I hope that's okay. I buried him on top of my mother's grave in the Rosehill Cemetery."

"Thank you, Michael," said Sadie softly as tears streamed down her face.

Michael took his handkerchief and gently wiped her tears. "Sadie this house belonged to Matthew and Esther Kirke. It was their dream to fill all these rooms with the voices of carefree children. But when that never happened they adopted me. I was three years old. My mother was a feisty little woman, tough as nails, just like you Sadie. She loved music and was Thompson's only piano teacher. She was determined that I become her prize student. I owe my love of music to her. Sadie, Doc Allison told me he believes you have suffered a severe head concussion and some form of amnesia. He said that sometimes it helps to restore memory by talking about it with a friend. If you feel like talking, I'd like to be that friend."

"Michael, I feel very blessed to have you as my friend."

"Sadie, I found a missing person poster that was sent out to all police departments thirteen years ago. I've also read many old newspaper articles. Sadie that missing person is you. Can you remember what happened on the evening of March 1st, 1909? You and your family were performing at a dance after a barn – raising near Gordonsville, Minnesota."

"Oh, Michael, I do remember my family. We loved making music together! Folks called us the Fiddle family, sometimes the Music-makers. Michael I've tried so hard to remember my family and now it's all coming back! Let's see, my sister's name is Sarai! We're identical twins. Oh, Michael we were inseparable, the very best of friends! And my mother's name is Rebekah. Oh, I've missed her so much! She was a wonderful mother! She always read the Bible to us at bedtime. She taught me how to pray, how to read, to cook, oh, she taught me everything. I owe my love of music to her! My father's name is Mark Stevens. Oh, Michael, my name is Sadie Savannah Stevens!" Sadie was overflowing with excitement! "We lived on a farm near Austin, Minnesota. My father raised Appaloosa horses. My grandparents lived just down the road. They are the ones who taught me the art of broom-making."

"Sadie, I'm so glad your memory has been restored. I hate to ask this of you. I know these memories may be very painful, but do you remember anything about the evening of your kidnap?"

"Well, after the dance mother and Sarai were trying to sober up Father. He'd had too much to drink. I told Mother, I'd start loading up our fiddles. I remember it was a really dark night, with no moon or stars. It was cold outside and there was snow on the ground. I heard someone coming up behind me, but before I could turn around they struck me over the head. When I woke up, I was blindfolded and tied to a mule. There was a heavy blanket over me. I felt like I was suffocating. I was so sick, the world was spinning and I kept throwing up. My head hurt so bad, I just wanted to die. I was on a train in a boxcar. I must have passed out again, because when I came too, I was tied to the bed in Oscar's cabin. I was so sick, dizzy and still throwing up. I remember begging Oscar for a drink and he just laughed with his heinous laughter. I was so frightened. I tried to pray to die, but I couldn't remember how. I didn't know who I was or where I was. I just couldn't remember anything. Oscar told me my drunk father had traded me for a mule. Since I was sick in bed, he had asked the preacher to come to the house to marry us. I didn't remember getting married, but I just couldn't remember anything. I was desperate for answers, but I only knew what Oscar told me. But after my head healed, I started to remember songs and scriptures I had memorized as a child. It helped me to deal with my depression. After Sarah was born, I didn't feel so alone. Oscar told me, I didn't know how to read and write. But one day I found an old cookbook. I guess it belonged to Oscar's mother, because the name in it was Nora Vage. I was so thankful, I could read it."

"Sadie, did you ever see the marriage license?"

"No, when I asked Oscar about it, he told me to mine my own business. I couldn't read it anyway."

"Sadie, I have searched the records. No marriage to Oscar Vage is recorded. Your name is Sadie Savannah Stevens."

"You mean I'm not married to Oscar?"

"No, it was all a pack of lies!"

Sadie cried out joyfully! "Hallelujah, Amen!"

Chapter 26   Your Goose is Cooked

"Oscar, do you want to tell me what happened on the evening of March 1, 1909?" asked Sherriff Kirke.

"I ain't tellin' ye nothin'!" sneered Oscar.

"Well let me tell you what happened then. Oscar, I found this missing person poster. Do you recognize this beautiful girl? Let me read it to you. It says: *$5,000.00 Reward for the where-abouts of 14 year old Sadie Savannah Stevens. 5' 3", 103 lbs. Golden blonde hair and green eyes. Kidnapped near Gordonsville, Minnesota on the evening of March 1, 1909.* You Oscar had just inherited the Vage farm and you needed a slave girl. You saw this beautiful young girl playing her fiddle at a barn-raising dance. If you're going to kidnap a slave, you figured you might as well get one easy on the eyes. And you started scheming with your evil, criminal mind; treachery of the worst sort! Oh, you pretend to be stupid, but it's a cover-up for your laziness. Everyone feels sorry for poor Oscar Vage. His elevator does not go all the way to the top, so we must let him off the hook. You may have fooled them all, but you have not fooled me. You are really smart; smart enough to plan a kidnap and cover your tracks for thirteen years. Smart enough to plaster over your wicked deeds like a whitewash fence!"

"Ye can't prove nothin'!" snarled Oscar. "I'm leavin'!"

"Oh, no you are not! We are not finished yet; we've only just begun! Oscar you are not just evil, you are incorrigibly wicked, the Devil in disguise! You snuck up behind Sadie and knocked her over the head. Oscar you did not trade your mule for Sadie; you used it to pack her battered body back home. You blindfolded her, tied her to your mule, threw a blanket over her and loaded them onto a boxcar all under the cloak of darkness. You saw Sadie's father drinking that night, so you started creating your cock-in-bull story. It was a believable story, because drunks don't know what they say or do."

"I giv' Sadie youn'uns," protested Oscar.

"She never asked you too! You abused that sweet girl, physically, emotionally, mentally and spiritually! You worthless weasel! **You selfishly took away thirteen years of that young girl's life!!!**" Michael slammed his fist down on his metal desk and sent papers flying everywhere!

"She's mi vife," yelled Oscar. "Sadie mi properte!"

"You are one sick puppy! Oscar, slavery was abolished in 1865 with the 13th Amendment. Sadie never was and never will be your wife or property! Her name is Sadie Stevens!"

"No, it ain't! It's Sadie Vage. She needs me. Sadie ain't smart enof to feed dose youn'uns vith out me!"

"Sadie has provided for her children for twelve years. She farmed the land, took care of the livestock, made brooms and willow baskets, while you selfishly spent your money at the tavern. Strutting around town in your new clothes and fancy boots. Tell me Oscar, how many pairs of shoes did you buy for your children? Did you ever buy them clothes, a peppermint stick, a toy, anything at all? No, you threatened, beat them, and let them go hungry and naked! **You are not a father!!!** You denied them of an education and now, you are going to sign over the deed to your farm to those children."

"In a pig's eye!" shouted Oscar.

"You, Oscar, are not going to need it where you are going. Oscar Vage you are charged with premeditated attempted manslaughter, kidnapping a minor and then crossing a state line, rape and torture—need I go on! Oh, wait, the fiddle David found hidden in the barn belonged to Sadie Stevens, didn't it Oscar? So let's add stealing to your list of charges." Michael shook his jail keys! "The evidence is undeniable! **Oscar Vage your goose is cooked!!!**"

~~~~~~

"Sadie, I would like to sign over the deed to my house to you and your children."

"Michael, I could never take your inheritance."

"Well then, do me a favor. Sit down at the piano. Do you know the tune to 'Daisy'?"

"Ja," nodded Sadie.

"Then please play." Michael sang, *"Sadie, Sadie, give me your answer do. I'm half-crazy all for the love of you. It won't be a stylish marriage, I can't afford a carriage. But you'll look sweet upon my horse, 'cuz there's plenty of room for two."* Michael got down on his knees. "Sadie, I'm asking you to be my bride. Please say yes!"

Sadie looked at her children. All eight heads were nodding up and down like bobbins with a big fish on the line. "Yes, Michael Kirke, I would love to be your bride!"

A chorus of happy voices cried out spontaneously from Sadie and Michael's children, filling every corner of the house. Then Michael took Sadie into his strong arms and kissed her tenderly. And Sadie felt the scars on her broken heart start to mend. For the first time in thirteen years, Sadie's heart was truly at peace!

Chapter 27   "I do!"

Alice Beatrice Hoversten woke up to a bright Indian summer day. It was Monday, October 30, 1922, and today she would marry her beloved friend, Palmer Olai Helgren.
The Hoverstens arose early to get ready for this special day.
"Chores aur dun," announced Ed washing up at the washstand.
"Kin't vait to see Anna an' gran'datters," replied Tobia. "Martin meet dem at da train depo'."
"Mother make sure you have your dress." Alice had made Tobia a new dress of wine-colored calico with a pink crocheted collar.
"Dun't vorry, I got rite here in mi satchel."
Alice loaded up the baskets of fresh rolls they had baked Sunday afternoon. "We better get going. Martin and Jennie may need some help."
"Nei, Jennie jist lik' ye; she be'n rede fer a veek or two," chuckled Ed starting up his truck.
The trip to Williams, Iowa, displayed tints of autumn everywhere. The elms and birch trees were tinged with yellow and the oaks with reddish-brown. The road ditches were full of blazing star, golden rod, Indian-pipe and ladies-tresses. The sunflowers seemed to hold their gorgeous faces up to be kissed by the sun.
Ed blasted the Klaxon to announce their arrival, **"Oogah! Oogah!"** as he turned into the Thompson's driveway.
As promised, Jennie had covered her flowerbeds to protect them from frost and they still were ablaze with color.
On the front porch stood Anna and her husband, Michael Risa with their five children.
"Children growin' lik' veeds!" chuckled Ed.
"Ja, Amy is ten, Olaf eight, Thelma seven, Elmer six and Mildred one," announced Anna.
The children gathered around Ed, Tobia and Alice to share hugs and kisses.
"How wuz da train rid'?" asked Ed.
Olaf answered, "Grandfather, it was great!"
Elmer added, "Ja, but we wanted it to go faster!"
"Of course ye did," chuckled Ed. "Boys vill be boys!"
"Looks lik' da Bervens aur here," announced Tobia.
"I gues' Hawkin finally giv' in and buy a motorkar," chuckled Ed.
" Hawkin, what kind of motorcar is that?" asked Michael.

"It's a 1917 Model T Touring-car. It has lots of space for our growing family," laughed Hawkin.
"That's what we need," said Michael.
"Uncle Hawkin, does it go faster than the train?" asked Olaf.
Hawkin answered, "I believe it does, son. After the wedding we'll take a ride and find out."
Inger handed Eunice to Grandmother Tobia and gave Alice a hug. "Ye sure picked a byutifel day for y'r wedding."
"Ja, I'm intoxicated with all this sunshine, fresh air, hugs and kisses," giggled Alice.
Inger gave her sister Anna a big hug. "Sure do miss ye!"
"Ye look very happy! Does motherhood agree with ye?" asked Anna.
"Ja, I lov' being a mother. Eunice just turned one and Allen is two. He follows Hawkin lik' a shadow," smiled Inger.
"Michael did ye git y'r crops out?" asked Hawkin.
"Ja, we had a nice fall and a bumper crop this year. I started plowing last week; I just love turning over that rich Minnesota soil," remarked Michael.
"Ye be all ready for spring planting," added Martin.
"Here com's mor' Hoverstens," chuckled Ed. "Jacob yust buy dat Roadster. It a nic' lukin' motorkar."
Ardis came running to the porch,"Onkel Martin, we got a Tin Lizzie, too!"
"You sure did," returned Martin, "she's a beauty!"
"Martin, you started this, giving us all 'tin lizzie fever'," laughed Jacob.
Edna put baby Norrene into Tobia's waiting arms.
Elmer shook his nephew's hand, "Hello, Elmer Risa!"
"Hello, Uncle Elmer," giggled Elmer.
Josie gave Alice a hug. "The bride to be looks beautiful. You are just glowing inside and out!"
"I'm gloating with all this delightful attention," giggled Alice.
Jennie was at the door hollering, "C'mon in!"
"Martin, goodt ye got a big haus'!" exclaimed Ed.
The Thompson's house was artistically decorated in pink and white with beautiful bouquets of flowers everywhere. Martin had removed the furniture from the parlor and living room, replacing it with benches for the guests.
Soon the Helgren family arrived. John, Palmer, Clarence and Leonard joined the men who were discussing farming, livestock, tractors and trucks.
"This is my sister, Lizzie," announced Martha.
"I'm so glad you were able to come," said Alice.

"I would not have missed it for anything!" exclaimed Palmer's aunt.
Martha and Lizzie set up the three tiered cake decorated with tiny pink roses.
"Dat's byutifel!" complimented Tobia. "Too purte to eat!"
"I'm sure the men won't agree," laughed Lizzie.
Alice gave Martha a big hug, "I love it! It's so pretty! It must have been a lot of work. The roses look so real."
"I'm thrilled to do it for Palmer and his new bride," stated Martha.
"Aunt Lizzie, Palmer and I would like you to cut the cake," said Alice.
"Oh Alice, thank you so much! I would be honored," exclaimed Lizzie.
The women all set to work on the bounteous wedding feast to be served at five o'clock. They would be serving ham, turkey, mashed potatoes and gravy, stuffing, Swedish meatballs and noodles, beans, corn, rolls, fruit salad and of course the beautiful wedding cake.
Alice and Hazel slipped into a bedroom to fix their hair and get dressed. Hazel handed Alice a package. Inside was a nightgown embroidered with tiny white daisies. "Thank you Hazel, it's so beautiful!" exclaimed Alice.
More wedding guests were arriving. Walter Carson, the best man and his wife Mary arrived with their new baby boy. Eli and Rachel were with them followed by the Kirke family. Jake Anderson and his wife Kristen followed and then the rest of Palmer's threshing crew, Bjorn Livingston, Hans Peterson and Olaf Hanson.
Jennie poked her head into the bedroom. "The minister is here are you ready?"
"Coming," said Alice with fluttering butterflies in her stomach.
Palmer and Walter stood at the front of the parlor dressed in navy blue suits, white shirts and the silk ties made by Alice. Lizzie had pinned on their white daisy bootineers. Hazel started down the aisle in a navy blue A-line dress with front and back princess seams. Tobia had added pink folkloric embroidery around the neckline and sleeves. She carried a bouquet of ferns and pink roses.
Michael and Sadie Kirke sang 'O, Perfect Love!' accompanied by David Kirke playing the piano.
As Ed took Alice's arm he whispered, "ye luk byutifel doter."
Alice had made a navy blue suit of fine linen. The princess seamed jacket had a matching A-line skirt. She carried a large bouquet of ferns with pink and white roses. In the center of the bouquet was one white daisy added by the groom.
Palmer saw Ed and Alice coming down the aisle and his heart was leaping for joy! He wanted nothing more than to spend the rest of his days loving his beloved bride. Palmer took Alice's hand and she gazed into his blue eyes. In their

reflection she saw all their dreams coming true. Palmer and Alice exchanged vows of love making them partners for life in a bond that would last as long as life itself. The minister pronounced the impressive words that joined the happy young couple, "Meet Mr. and Mrs. Palmer Helgren. You may kiss the bride."

Alice blushed at the thought of kissing in front of family and friends, but Palmer was not bashful. He had restrained himself for so long, a team of wild horses were not going to hold him back, not even a second longer. Palmer was ready to give them full rein! Palmer smothered Alice in his embrace and gave her a passionate kiss! The audience all applauded with enthusiasm!

John whispered, "what a handsome pair."

Martha returned, "so much in love."

The newlyweds sat down to open their gifts.

When they unwrapped the rolling pin, Ed chuckled, "Palmer, ye bet'er vatch out!"

Next came a large cast iron frying pan.

John advised, "better stay plumb out of the kitchen, Palmer!"

Snickers came from the wedding guests!

They opened Tobia's green and gold creamer and sugar bowl. "It cam' al' da vay 'cross da oshen. How it git here vith no chip, ve never 'no'!"

There was china, silverware, a vase, a recipe book, dishtowels, sheets, a quilt, a sideliner broom and willow basket, a poetry book and a large Bible.

"There's plenty of space in the front to write down all the names of your children," said Aunt Lizzie.

"Ve kud not bring aur gift, cuz it too big," explained Ed. "Ve took it to Palmer's haus'."

"You'll love it Alice!" exclaimed Palmer. "It's an oak table with ten chairs."

"Got big famle, need big tabl'," added Ed.

"Does that mean you'll come for supper quite often?" asked Alice.

"Ye kin count on dat!" smiled Ed.

"Count us in!" cried Jacob and Elmer in unison.

John handed Palmer an envelope. "We couldn't agree on a gift so we decided to give money, instead. You can get whatever you need."

Palmer replied, "I can't think of a thing I need. I'm blessed with a wonderful family, true friends and now a beloved wife! If I were to ask for anything more, I'd be a selfish man."

"I dink da boy be a poet som'day lik' his bride," chuckled Ed.

The room filled with happy laughter from the wedding guests!

"You have all worked so hard to make this day special for us," said Alice. "Your precious gifts bring tears to my eyes. I will cherish this day always! The memory of your smiles, laughter and loving support will hold a special place in my heart forever!"

Palmer added, "Thank you all for sharing this special day with us. We so appreciate your wonderful gifts, but having our loved ones around us today is the greatest gift of all!"

"No more speeches," announced Eli. "I'm about to cry crocodile tears!"

The wedding guests roared with laughter!

Chapter 28 Telltale Signs

Frosty mornings brought an end to autumn's rainbow of colors. Foliage of russet, brown and gold covered the ground. The air had turned cool and crisp. The cutting north wind rustled among the pines as smoke rose from the chimneys. One could not ignore the approach of winter as the days began to shorten. Nestled among the trees was the white farmhouse that Alice now called home. She stayed busy sewing curtains for all the windows and baking Palmer's favorite meals. Being Palmer's new bride exceeded the imaginations of Alice's heart! Palmer had brought all the livestock into the barns. The woodshed was full of firewood. Palmer came in the back door, hung up his coat and pulled off his boots. Coming home to Alice always gave Palmer a cozy warm feeling that flooded his whole body from the inside out!

Alice was just taking her bread out of the oven.

"Alice your bread smells as wonderful as it tastes!" Palmer hurried over to the cook-stove. "The thought of coming home to you always warms my heart."

"I wish it would warm your hands, too. Mr. Helgren, don't you dare touch me with those icy hands of yours!"

"My beloved bride, you are an expert at warming them up." Palmer drew Alice into his arms and kissed her tenderly. "I've waited all day for that! My love for you is as deep and unfathomable as the night sky."

"You are becoming quite the poet, Romeo," giggled Alice. She felt so content nestled in Palmer's embrace. His endearing love chased away the darkness of the long winter nights. "Palmer, are you hungry?"

"Ja, I'm starving!"

"Well, maybe we should get the chicken pot pie out of the oven before it burns."

"So that's what smells so good! I'll get it Alice." Palmer grabbed the pot holders. "I talked to Gunvor at the Blacksmith Shop today. He said he'd sell us a milk cow if you want one."

"Oh, Palmer, we could have fresh-churned butter every day. Ja, and ice cream, too!"

"I'll take that as a yes."

Alice started slicing her bread. "So what's the weather doing out there?"

"The temperature is dropping, the wind picking up and the clouds are laden with snow. It's sure to dump on us again before morning. I gathered all the eggs I could find, because I knew they would freeze during the night."

"I don't mind being snowed in as long as I'm with you," came Alice's sweet reply.

"Guess what I heard today?"
"Eli and Rachel are engaged," giggled Alice.
"Who told you?"
"Rachel did. She stopped by today with that big pile of fabric. She has a new idea for saving her premature babies."
"And where did she get this idea from?"
"From a kangaroo pouch."
"What?"
"We designed a bag for new mothers. We're going to call it the 'joey pouch'." Rachel thinks the babies will have a better chance of survival if they stay warm, can hear their mother's heartbeat and nurse more often."
"What will you girls think of next?" laughed Palmer. "I dropped off the clothes you sewed for the Kirke children. Young David has three violin students. He's saving his money for a bicycle. Sadie has so many piano students she can't keep up. So her sister Sarai moved here to help out and Hans Peterson is head over heels in love with her. Olaf Hanson is courting Rachel's sister, Malenda. Karina Anderson has her bonnet set on Bjorn Livingston and Ole Torgenson is chasing Helga Huddelson."
"Oh, is she the fountain clerk at Johnson's Drug Store?"
"Ja, Ole's been drinking a lot of Dr Pepper lately," smiled Palmer.
"Oh my! Love is budding out everywhere and it's not even spring yet," giggled Alice as she dished up the pot pie. "I've got some news to share, too." Alice patted the telltale swelling under her tight dress.
"Alice that's the best news ever!"
Alice was back in Palmer's arms again and the chicken pot pie was getting cold.

Chapter 29   Skeeter

Soon the overladen branches dropped their white burden to the ground. The great snow drifts melted and winter's mournful, wailing wind ceased. The spring thaw of 1923 was finally here. Spring rains brought new blades of green grass that promised the return of life. Overhead geese flying north peppered the sky. Robins hopped around the yard pulling up worms. The flowering dogwood was budding and tulips and Iris poked through the soil. The wake-robin growing along the fence line was in full bloom. In the garden asparagus spears popped up daily. Alice made asparagus soup, creamed it, baked, fried and scrambled it with eggs. Palmer claimed if he ate another spear of that green stuff it would surely come out his ears. The long winter had made Alice fell like a caged bird. It felt so good to shake off the winter blues and spread her wings again. She had planted her cool weather plants in April. Alice had worried the frost might still come to visit, but her lettuce, radishes, onions, corn, potatoes, peas, carrots, broccoli, cauliflower and cabbage were all up and thriving. Palmer had headed to the field early each morning believing that the early bird gets the worm. If all went well, he should finish planting the corn today. The garden was calling Alice, but she needed to get Daisy milked first. Alice bent beneath the Guernsey cow and pulled her milk stool under her as she pressed her head into Daisy's flank. Frothy, warm milk went singing into her metal pail.

"Keep your tail to yourself Daisy," warned Alice.

Tiger, the barn cat appeared and waited patiently for a squirt of milk.

"Tiger open up wide," ordered Alice as she sent a squirt his way. Alice missed her target and hit the cat in the eye. "Sorry Tiger," giggled Alice.

Tiger didn't seem to mind as he used his long tongue to clean out his eye.

Alice turned Daisy out to pasture and carried her milk to the house. It seemed that work loomed around every corner. *Where should I start?* There was butter to churn, bread to bake and clothes to wash. Here it was the 10th of May already; she better finish planting the garden. Alice raked the soil. She loved the smell of fresh turned earth. Alice listened to the song of a wren serenading her from the apple tree. The warmth of the sun felt so good on her face. She stuck a stick at the end of the new row and unwound her string until she reached the other side of the garden. Alice dug a furrow along the string and dropped her green bean seeds into the soil. She pushed the seeds into the ground with her barefoot. Alice planted cucumbers, squash, peppers and tomatoes. She robbed a few potatoes from their underground home, a couple carrots and a onion. Potato soup would go well with her sourdough bread. Alice stoked the morning, red coals with kindling. There was no oak or locust left in the wood-box and she preferred it for baking bread which needed a steady, hot fire. Palmer had promised to replenish the woodpile after the planting season. Surely she could find a few logs to split. There was no oak left, but she found some hickory and ash. It would have to do. Alice set a piece of ash on the chopping block. She swung the ax and it made a **"thud"** as it split the ash log. The ax blade was dull.

Father always says a dull ax uses far too much muscle. His favorite saying is, "Work smarter, not harder!"

Alice went to the toolshed to find a file to hone the blade. Alice set another log on the chopping block and with one mighty **"whack"** the crunch of splitting hickory rang through the air. She picked up a chunk of wood, **"whack, and crunch!"** **"Whack, crunch!"** Alice's pile of wood was steadily growing. Suddenly a searing pain gripped Alice's womb and she gasped for her next breath! She dropped to the chopping block to rest.

It's too early for the baby to come. Rachel warned me about false labor. She said sometimes the uterus likes to practice before the real event.

Alice used her apron to wipe the sweat from her forehead. She walked to the pump to get a cool drink. Then she gathered up her split wood. Alice was caught off guard as her next contraction rolled over her and she collapsed on the porch steps. Once inside the house she loaded her wood into the cook-stove and placed her bread in the oven. She needed to get the soup started. Palmer would be coming in from the field soon. She went to the sink and started scrubbing her potatoes and carrots as another spasm stabbed her womb. Alice heard Max barking and then a **"knock"** at the front door.

Alice cried out, "Come in!"

Rachel could see the fear in Alice's eyes. Pain was etched on her face. "Are you okay?"

"I'm getting a taste of false labor today."

"Alice, go lay down. I'll finish your soup."

Alice stood up and felt something wet running down her legs, making a puddle on the kitchen floor.

"Alice, your labor is real. Your baby is on the way."

~~~~~~

Palmer returned from the field and saw the ax next to the chopping block.

That's my job. When will Alice learn, she's not a man! He picked up a piece of evidence and started toward the house.

Rachel met Palmer at the back door. "Alice is in labor."

Palmer dropped his piece of split ash in disbelief. "Nei, it's too early! Can't you stop it?"

"Her water broke. There's no stopping it now. The baby's on the way. Did you make a birth-chair?"

"It's in the barn."

"Get it and hurry! Palmer giving birth is like swimming up river against a raging current! I need your help!"

The severity of Alice's pains increased. Palmer kissed Alice's sweating brow. Her face was flushed with exertion, etched with pain and fatigue. Her eyes were full of worry and desperation!

Fear gripped Palmer's heart as he reached for Alice's hand. "My beloved Alice, I love you so much! I wish I could take your pain! Be courageous and strong, my little daisy in the wheat field!"

Alice nodded. She was too exhausted to respond. Intense pain ravaged her body with every labored breath! Writhe spasms of horrendous pain grew stronger and stronger as her time drew near! Her breaths came in gasps! Palmer helped her pant through each excruciating contraction, reminding her of his love and the little one they would soon hold in their arms. Soon Alice felt the uncontrollable urge to push!

"Palmer help me get Alice on the birth chair."

Alice felt like every ounce of her strength was spent, but her muscles were bearing down with an iron-like-will of their own! A wee little pink head appeared and Ernest slid into Rachel's waiting hands. First a weak whimper and then a red-faced squall! Rachel wrapped the wee one tightly in a warm blanket. Alice's anguish was forgotten with little Ernie in her arms.

"He's no bigger than a skeeter with duck-fluff for hair," claimed his proud father.

Chapter 30   **"Hiyah!"**

Marvin was born May 9, 1925. Alice was as busy as a hungry bear in berry season! Two year old Ernie had a torrent of questions coming out of his little mouth. There was no end to his vitality. He loved Palmer's rough-housing and thrived on silliness. Ernie followed Palmer like a shadow and cried when Palmer went to work in the field.
"Me go, p'eas!" pouted Ernie.
Palmer tousled Ernie's cornsilk hair. "You're the big brother now. You need to help Mommy take care of baby Marvin."
"I wanna go," cried Ernie with a quivering chin.
"You'll be fine," assured Alice. "Let's get your pants on and cover up those scrawny chicken legs."

~~~~~~

When I get done planting, I need to get that fence up along the road. There's always too much to do and never enough time to do it. Palmer harnessed his two Percheron draft horses, Rex and Jess. They were a well-matched pulling team. Palmer took the reins and hollered, **"Hiyah!"** as they headed for the field. Palmer hitched his team to the plow and looped the lines over his shoulder. **"Hiyah!"** he called as he slapped the reins on the horse's rumps urging them forward. The plow blade cut through the rich Iowa soil as they moved down the field. The strong, clean smell of the earth slowly rolled over as the horses set their labored pace. Rex and Jess plodded along with the warm May sunshine bearing down. Palmer's shirt soon darkened with sweat. They made a trip up the field and back, up and back, turning over miles of fresh plowed soil.

~~~~~~

Alice changed Marvin's diaper and put him back in his 'joey-pouch'. She took Ernie by the hand. "Let's go feed the chickens." Alice had two dozen Brahma laying hens. They were meaty birds and could survive cold winters. A good choice for northern Iowa. Alice earned "pin money" by selling the eggs for cash or credit at Erickson's General Store. The chickens were free-roaming during the day. When they saw Ernie with his little pail of corn, they all came cackling and running across the yard. Alice noticed that the wind was picking up. The gilded

weathervane on the big, white barn was spinning like a top. The vibration of the wind-swept windmill seemed to shake the ground. The temperature was dropping and dark, swirling clouds with an odd greenish tinge loomed above. The forceful, deafening wind knocked Ernie down and he spilled his pail of corn.
"Mommy my corn!" he wailed.
The chickens were running for cover! Not even the pile of spilled corn could tempt them. The powerful wind swirled dirt into their eyes. Marvin was crying from his 'joey-pouch'. Alice grabbed Ernie around the waist and ran toward the house.

~~~~~~

Palmer looked anxiously at the dark clouds building up in the angry sky. The tall willow trees along the fence line bent and swayed like mighty giants tossing their wild arms about. A ragged bird's nest which had once burdened the higher branches of an oak tree, drifted away upon the swirling wind. The rumble of thunder gave a distant warning! Palmer pulled his straw hat down tighter. He didn't feel like chasing a flying hat today. The temperature was dropping quickly. Another roll of thunder forecast threatening rain or worse yet, hail. The horses grew more and more restless. **"Whoa! Easy boys!"** Palmer brought the team to a halt. He hurried to unhitch the plow. The draft horses were impatient, stamping and sidling about with snorts and quivering ears. Their long, brown manes and tails were whipped about like clothes on a line. Palmer spoke in a low voice trying to calm them. The powerful wind increased emitting a deafening roar. Palmer's hat sailed away like a mighty ship at full mast. Swirling gusts whipped all around them. Palmer struggled to keep his footing as if the very earth were heaving! Branches torn from the trees shot pass them like arrows released from a bow! Palmer tried to shield his eyes while clinging to the horses. They were caught in a dangerous black blizzard! The dirt stung Palmer's cheeks and filled his eyes, while grit covered his lips! *We've got to get back to the barn!* He took up the reins again and screamed, **"Haw!"** trying to turn the team to the left. Then Palmer saw a long, narrow twisting funnel. He shrieked, **"Gee!"** trying to turn the team back to the right. **"HIYAH!!! HIYAH!!! HIYAH!!!"** The team lunged forward as he drove them down into the deep road ditch, thankful that he'd never had time to put up the fence! Palmer grabbed for the lines just under the horses' bits and hung onto them with all his strength!

Alice sat on the bottom step of the stairs in the cellar with Marvin and Ernie in her arms. She poured out her heart praying that Palmer would survive this terrible storm! The cellar door opened and Alice spun around with relief. There stood Palmer covered with black dirt from head to toe. "Mr. Palmer Olai Helgren, I can see you're in desperate need of some soap and hot water!"

Chapter 31   Alice's Wit

Alice did not like Palmer's new hired man. His name was Nabal Zinnser and he had bought the old Vage farm. After Oscar's monstrous behavior, Alice felt it was best to lean toward the cautious side. Nabal was the oddest old duffer Alice had ever seen. He was a tall, rough-looking character with the leathery face of a desperado and a long scar on his left cheek. Nabal had stormy, coal black eyes and long shaggy hair, black as a raven. His long face, creased by wind and weather wore a black, unkempt, scraggly beard. He wore a long wolf skin coat and a battered old sombrero. Alice was sure he was a bootlegger. He had the perfect place to set up a moonshine-still along the creek in those thick woods. And Alice had seen smoke rising from his woods during the night, when she got up to nurse Marvin. Alice found it a little peculiar that he raised corn, yet never sold it and had little livestock. Palmer agreed that Nabal was a little strange, but a bootlegger, really Alice. Nabal was a strong, hard worker and Palmer claimed they needed his help. Palmer had over 400 acres to farm and Alice had her hands full with two small children and a huge garden.

Palmer and Nabal had just finished building a new farrowing house. The weather was turning cold and now it was time to get the sows in there before the new piglets arrived.

Alice was just taking another pan of biscuits out of the oven when the men came in for supper.

"Smells good in here, Ma'am. I bet ya missed me lik' a bad itch!" Then Nabal's stern face crumbled into laughter. "I 'bout gone fer hunger!" he exclaimed has he flopped into a chair.

Palmer played with Marvin who was in the highchair. "Son, you're supposed to put the food in your mouth, not in your hair," laughed Palmer. Marvin smiled and touched his messy hand to his head adding another layer of gravy to his hair.

Palmer dropped into a kitchen chair next to Ernie who was enjoying his biscuit and sausage gravy. "We're plumb exhausted from chasing Clementine! That old sow is as ornery as they come! She's obstinate, ill-tempered and downright mean! She charged at Max and tried to bite him!"

"Daddy is Max okay?" asked Ernie.

"He's fine! Max is way too fast for Clementine. She's slow and heavy with all those piglets inside."

"Yup! That big mama is loaded down," blurted Nabal. "Those Chester White sows like Clementine can realle pump out piglets." Nabal always seemed to be an expert on all subjects. "Palmer what is she bred too?"
"A Black Bershire."
"I s'pose the piglets be black and white then," said Nabal scratching his beard. "I'd almost wager on it."
Ernie inquired, "If Clementine is slow, how come you can't catch her?"
"That thar little chap, he dun't miss a thing!" Nabal roared with laughter as he wiped his milk mustache on his ragged sleeve. Then he swallowed another biscuit in two gulps. "Your wife, a mite fine cook," mumbled Nabal as he reached for another biscuit with his big, calloused hands. "Mmm..."
How would he know if I'm a good cook? He never takes the time to taste anything. The way he wolfs his food down is a disgrace!
Nabal was gulping down his third glass of milk. "Mmm...ain't nuthin' bet'er 'cept maybe a jug of corn licker!"
Alice flashed Palmer an I-told-you-so look!
"Yes-sum, I reckon ya can't find vittles any bet'er no mat'er how far ya roam."
Ernie asked, "Daddy are the new piglets here?"
"Not yet, it won't be long though. Pocahontas is making a nest with the straw. That's a good sign she's almost ready to have her babies. Tillie, Matilda and Pocahontas walked right in and lay down in their pens. But Clementine refuses to go in her new house. She headed for the woods and led us right through a quagmire of mud. Up and down and around and around. Nothing seems to work," laughed Palmer. "Maybe we'll have to get Sheriff Kirke to help us. That man can track a feather in a dust storm."
"Naw, I don't car' a whit for hogs. Ain't got one on the place. I got bet'er things to do with my corn then waste it on those stinkin' stubborn critters. But I do lik' pork chops an' ham. Ya, 'no' what they say, 'the only thing wasted on a pig is the squeal!'" Then Nabal roared with laughter at his own wisecrack. "Yup, I'm plumb fed up," yellow teeth flashed as Nabal spoke. "We be'n trapsin al'over this here farm after that ol' sow. I'm mad enof to spit nails! We be chasin' her till doomsday. No use frettin' 'bout it. That ornery critter ain't goin' in that thar farrowin' house. Nosirree! Our best bet is to turn her into bacon."
"You can't drive a hog," stated Alice as she cleaned up Marvin with a wash cloth and handed him to Palmer. She had seen Clementine rutting along her garden fence from the kitchen window.

"Ma'am, I s'pose you know al' 'bout hogs," blurted Nabal with his husky voice. "They ain't lik' chickens, ya can't jist say,'Shoo! Shoo!'"

Ernie was pulling on his coat. "I wanna go see the pigs!"

Alice stuck a couple biscuits in her apron pocket. She tossed Nabal a glare as she said, "You have to be smarter than a hog before you can do anything with one." She grabbed her coat and headed out the back door. The men grabbed their coats and followed. Palmer zipped baby Marvin inside his coat with him.

Nabal was pulling on his muddy boots. "I'd like to put a little wager on this," he spouted. "She ain't gonna do nuthin' with that thar rebellious hog! Yup, women got 'bout as much sense as a hog."

Alice threw a piece of biscuit to Clementine and she gobbled it right down. Then Alice dropped a biscuit trail all the way to the farrowing house. Clementine followed along at Alice's heels, wolfing down bits of Alice's delicious biscuits. Alice led Clementine right into her pen and closed the gate. Clementine rutted some straw into a corner and lay down.

"Well, I'll be," declared Nabal scratching his beard. "Iffen I was to wager on that thar deal, I woulda lost my shirt! Who'da thout? I'm downright baffled! I larn a heap today! This is a fine how-do-you-do! I've been out smarted by an old sow and one smart woman!"

~~~~~~

Pocahontas had a fine litter of ten piglets. Tillie followed with eleven and Matilda had thirteen. But irritable, grumpy old Clementine out did them all with a litter of sixteen!

"We got that farrowing house up just in time," remarked Palmer as he trudged through the snow carrying Ernie. Alice followed through the first snow of the year carrying Marvin on her hip. As Palmer opened the door they were greeted with the grunts of nursing mamas and the squeals of little piglets.

"Clementine might be an ill-natured sow, but she is a good mother," praised Alice. Palmer reached in the pen and grabbed the little white runt. "I'm going to name this one, Biscuit."

"Let me hold heem," begged Ernie.

Palmer placed the squirming piglet in Ernie's arms. "You might have to feed him with a bottle."

"O, goody!" said Ernie with delight.

"He's pig-ugly!" exclaimed Alice.

"Dat's what mak' heem so-o cute," giggled Ernie.

Chapter 32   The Photograph

Summer of 1926

"Alice your Komla was so delicious," remarked Martha. "Mine never tastes that good. Palmer is a blessed man for sure!"
"Well the credit should go to Mother. She taught me everything I know."
"I not 'no' much, but von never forget how to kuk," laughed Tobia.
"I alvays say, 'kiss the kuk, she's Norwegian,'" chuckled Ed.
"That has become one of my favorite sayings," agreed Palmer winking at Alice.
"Mine too," said Jacob and Elmer in unison.
"Ye two is a kupl' of bot'omles' pits," spouted Tobia. "Dun't 'no' how Edna and Josie kin ke'p up!"
Hawkin complimented, "Inger is an excellent cook. She was trained by the best."
"Anna too," added Michael.
"I hope you saved room for Jennie's chocolate cake," announced Alice.
"I'll have to wait until later," exclaimed John. "I couldn't even fit another crumb in right now."
"Palmer, how many acres are you farming now?" asked Michael.
"Four hundred, that's why I bought the new tractor," explained Palmer. "I still use Rex and Jess for small jobs. I don't have the heart to sell them."
"I'd like to get a look at that tractor," said Martin.
Three year old Ernie hollered, "Me too!"
"He'd live on that tractor if we'd let him," laughed Palmer.
The men all headed outside to see the new iron-wheel tractor. Little Ernie led the way followed by an entourage of cousins, Olaf and Elmer Risa, Allen Berven, Ardis, Raymond and Robert Hoversten. Grandpa John Helgren carried Marvin and Michael Risa carried Arlen.
"Well those men sure do know when it's dishwashing time," laughed Martha.
"Many hands lighten the load," remarked Jennie.
"Josie dis lit'l felo git hungre," said Grandma Tobia, handing Leslie to his mother. "Heem rede to nurs'."
"Mother, Ethel is getting hungry, too. She's sucking on her hand," said fourteen year old Amy, handing over her new sister.
"Our many hands are dropping like flies," giggled Alice.
Josie asked, "When was Ethel born?"
"The 3rd of April," answered Anna.

"Leslie was born the 13th of March. He's only two weeks older than Ethel, but look how big he is," stated Josie.

"He jist lik' his fader," explained Tobia. "Elmer nurs' lik' a pig an' heem stil' eat lik' von! How heem sta' so thin? I dun't 'no'!"

"Amy and Thelma, why don't ye take the little ones outside to play?" suggested Anna.

"There's a swing hanging from the oak tree," reported Alice.

Eleven year old Thelma carried two year old Vivian. Amy took the hand of three year old Helen and offered her other hand to four year old Norrene. The five year olds, Mildred and Eunice followed.

"Alice, your garden is beautiful," replied Jennie looking out the kitchen window. "I love the colorful border of zinnas!"

"Don't look to close," sighed Alice. "It's the garden of weedin'!"

"It's hard to keep up with two little ones," said Edna sympathetically. "Ardis watches Norrene and Raymond for me, but I can't expect too much from a six year old."

"Palmer ordered a toy tractor for Ernie from the Sears Roebuck catalogue. Ernie farms right down the middle of my vegetable rows, but I have to keep Marvin in the buggy. He puts everything in his mouth."

"Raymond's past that stage, but now we're in the terrible-twos," sighed Edna.

After the dishes were done, Alice took glasses and a pitcher of lemonade out to the men who had gathered on the front porch. Jennie served chocolate cake with buttercream frosting.

"Martin, ye aur a blessed man," chuckled Ed as he took another bite of cake.

"That I am," returned Martin as he looked lovingly at his wife Jennie.

Palmer and John set up the Croquet game. Amy, Thelma, Olaf, Elmer, Allen and Ardis all grabbed mallets and sent their wooden balls flying in all directions. Ernie brought out his box of wooden blocks and the younger cousins built towers, just to knock them down and start all over again.

"I brought my new Kodak camera. Would you like me to take a family photograph?" offered John.

"I vud luv dat!" exclaimed Tobia.

"Well, the babies are up from their naps," explained Anna.

Josie added, "this would be a good time."

Ed announced, "Everyvon find y'r youn'uns. Ve tak' famle picsure. Anna an' Michael git in bak row. Amy and Olaf stand in front of folks. Dat luks goodt. Now Thelma and Elmer, oh kin't see Olaf's fac'. Elmer, I dink ye grew a kupl' inch fram dat big din'er ve ate. Bet'er mov' over so ve kin see y'r broder's fac'. O, dat's bet'er. Now ve put Mildred, Helen and Arlen in front row."

"O, Arlen not sta'! Dere heem goes!" chuckled Tobia.

Michael chased after him and brought the squirming child back.

Ed asked, "Helen kin ye hold heem hand?"

"O, dere heem go, ag'in," chuckled Tobia.

"Michael, ye bet'er hold dat von. Goodt, dat tak' car' of Risa famle, Berven's next," sighed Ed.

"Vhat 'bout Ethel?" chuckled Tobia.

"O, I forgit da nu von! Dis kud tak' al' day!"

Palmer took two chairs off the porch. "Ed and Tobia sit here and everyone else gather around."

"Mother you can hold Ethel and Leslie," suggested Alice. "Father can hold Marvin and Arlen."

"Marvin rede fer a nap an' so is his gran'fader," chuckled Ed.

Alice sat the younger children on the grass in front of Tobia and Ed. "Now stay put!" she ordered.

"Ve ben bless vith mane gran'datters!" Tobia beamed with pride.

"Who invented the camera?" asked Martin. "Was his name Kodak?"

"Nei, that's not right. I saw it on the instruction manuel," explained John. "Martha, it's in the camera case."

Martha pulled it out of the case and announced, "the camera was invented by George Eastman right here in America in 1888."

"I'd like to tear it apart and see how it's made," stated Palmer.

"Oh, no you don't. This one is brand new!" exclaimed John.

"Where did ye get it?" asked Jacob.

"We ordered it from the Sears Roebuck catalogue," explained Martha.

"Does it work well?" asked Hawkin.

"This is my first photograph, so I'm trying to find out!" returned John patiently.

"Father can you see all 32 faces?" asked Palmer.

John answered, "Ja, it looks pretty good."

"Better hurry before another one gets away," laughed Martha.

"Okay, is everyone ready now," asked John.

Everyone shouted, "Ja!"

John announced, "I'm going to take the picture on the count of three. One, two..."

"Wait!" hollered little Ernie. "We forgot Max! Here boy, com' here Max!"

Everyone roared with laughter as Max joined the group.

"Okay, all 33 faces smile," shouted John. "Ready, one, two, three…"
"Click,click!"

Chapter 33   Blessed Rest

Alice's nerves were shattered by her frenzied obsessed search for Ernie. She was beyond frantic when the men came in for breakfast. "I can't find Ernie!"

"I got a hankerin', we ain't goin' to get no work dun today," complained Nabal. "Where hav' ye luked?"

Palmer suggested, "Let's call Max. Where Max is that's where you'll find Ernie. Palmer stepped outside and whistled for Max. They heard Max barking from the cow pasture. Palmer and Nabal took off running and Alice followed toting Marvin. Faithful Max was standing guard and Ernie was underneath Daisy with the milk pail. Daisy didn't seem to mind. She was content just standing there snatching mouthfuls of tender spring grass. In an instant, Palmer had drawn Ernie from his perilous position.

"Son, you can't go underneath cows, they might kick you!" exclaimed Palmer.

"I milkin' Daisy," explained Ernie.

"I alrede milked her. Thar ain't no milk in that thar udder!" howled Nabal. He pulled the milk pail out from under Daisy and peered inside. "Who'da thought," said Nabel scratching his beard. "I'll be jiggered, that thar lit'l chap has got a kupl' squirts of milk in this here pail. Ow-wee! That was down-writ' danjerous! I knowed a fello' got kicked in the head. He never was too bright after that thar happened!"

Alice thought, *so that's what happened to Nabal!*

Nabel babbled on, "I reckon this ain't a good way to start the day. Day's alrede rurnt an' my hair turin' gray." Then Nabal planted his feet as if he had grown right there in the pasture. He took off his old sombrero and scratched his head. "Tis bet'er than riches to scratch when it itches!" declared Nabal Zinnser.

Alice thought, *the man's stark-raving mad!!!*

"Ernie, we all learn some things the hard way," consoled Alice.

Palmer agreed, "Good judgment comes from experience and experience comes from bad judgment."

Nabal snatched the conversation back. "I reckon ye al' writ', but we ain't goin' to get nuthin' dun iffen we keep on jawin'! Ma'am I sur' got a hankerin, to put som' of y'r fin' vittles in this here growlin' belly of mine!"

Little Ernie agreed, "Mommy, I've worked up a man's appetite!"

"That thar lit'l chap is down-writ' funne," snorted Nabal.

After breakfast the men headed to the field to cultivate the corn and Alice went to the garden to rob a few potatoes for dinner.

Nabal snorts at his own corny jokes and eats like a hog, too, thought Alice. No matter how much Alice made, Nabal cleaned it up; to the last crumb of bread, to the last morsel of food, and to the last drop of milk.
I won't be surprised if I find the man licking his plate someday. Well no one can accuse him of wastefulness. Going into winter with empty canning jars would be bad judgment for sure! Alice sighed, "Why does Palmer always pick the hired men with the voracious appetites?"

~~~~~~

The men returned from the field to help with the evening chores. Nabal milked Daisy, Palmer slopped the hogs and Alice helped Ernie find the eggs.
"Mommy, can I carry the eggs," begged Ernie.
Alice had her arms full carrying Marvin, so she gladly handed over the egg basket. Things were going along quite well until Ernie tripped in a pot-hole and the eggs went sailing.
"Mommy, I hurt my knee," wailed Ernie. "The eggs are broke!"
"The hens will lay more eggs tomorrow," consoled Alice.
Palmer and Nabal came running!
"Son, you're supposed to let your mother scramble the eggs," teased Palmer.
"Who'da thout we'd hav' two mishaps in the sam' day," spouted Nabal. "Luk-ee here! One egg survived the crash." He popped it in his mouth shell and all.
He must be related to the mongoose family, thought Alice.
Nabal scratched his beard, "Lit'l chap ye bet'er be mor' keerful fram now on."
Palmer picked up Ernie. "Look, Max is lapping up the eggs, so they didn't go to waste after all."
"Yup, no use frettin' 'bout it. When eggs is broke that thar way, there jist ain't no repair to it," barked Nabal. "Life is sur' tuff. Ye sur' did a number on that thar knee lit'l chap. That's gonna itch lik' thunder when it starts to heal!" Nabal let out a big belch! "Gues' that thar egg went down sideways and hatched in my belly. I best git hom' fer I start crowin'. Iffen, I dun't drown in the creek, I be back in the mornin'." Nabel caught his mule which he had put out to pasture. "Whoa, mule, stand stil' thar," he shrilled. With one agile spring, Nabal easily landed on the back of his mule. "Giddap mule," coaxed Nabal trying to move the stubborn mule forward. "What ails you, ya ol' fool?" Nabal gave his mule a slap on the rump! "Get along thar, ya ol' nag!" The old mule lurched forward at her own slow, labored pace. Nabal's long legs dangled of the sides of the mule and barely

cleared the ground. As they plodded along Nabal sang: *"the chickens cackle an' the rooster crows it ain't-a gonna rain no mor' how in the heck kin I wash my neck if it ain't-a gonna rain no mor'..."*

Palmer and Alice swapped grins. Then their smiles broadened until a storm of laughter struck them!

When Palmer's laugh-attack was under control again, he choked out the words, "he's quite a character!"

"They don't come any loonier than that!" exploded Alice.

When Palmer recovered from his second fit of laughter, he said, "Alice, its been a long day. I think we should retire with the chickens tonight."

"I agree. I've got water heating on the stove in the bathhouse. You can get cleaned up and then I'll bring the boys."

~~~~~~

Alice put the boys in the tub with Palmer. "I'll be right back with more towels and pajamas."

When Alice returned, the bathhouse looked like a swamp from all the splashing. "It looks like you all love the water, so why do you throw it out of the tub? Has anyone grown a tail yet?"

"I need to unload a couple of little minnows," laughed Palmer. "Watch out Alice, they're slippery little fellows!"

When everyone was dried off and dressed, Palmer scooped a boy into each arm. "Come on boys, it's bedtime." Marvin gave a noisy yawn and his little head dropped on Palmer's shoulder. "Ernie you're nearly asleep as you stand."

"Nei, I not sleepy," said Ernie shaking his head. "Horsey ride, Daddy! Giddy-up! Eeeeee, aw!"

"Ernie this room is a mess! You are a big pack rat! **Ouch!!!**"

"Daddy did you step on something?"

"Ja, and I think the imprint is permanently branded on the bottom of my left foot. This room needs a 'proceed with caution' sign on the door."

"I hope you didn't step on my airplane!"

"Ernie, you need to quit thinkin' about pretty girls like your Mommy and get this place cleaned up."

~~~~~~

"Alice, I put the boys to bed when you were taking your bath."
"Thank you, my beloved. You are such a good husband and father!"
"Alice when I come home to you, I always find such a blessed sense of rest."
"Well we best get some sleep, the wee hours of the morning will come way too early."
"Ja, they always do," yawned Palmer.
Ernie hollered, "Daddy, lit'l broder is standing up in his crib!"
"So much for blessed rest," giggled Alice.
"Alice, you stay in bed. I'll take care of it."
"Marv, what are you babbling about? Did you wet your britches?" asked Palmer.
"Daddy, did he pee in his diaper?"
"Yup, it's soaked! Ernie pull that chamber pot out from under the bed."
"But I dun't hav' to go," protested Ernie.
"Well, I want you to try anyway."
"No pee-pee is comin' out."
"Give it some time. There's always some in there." Palmer sat down in the rocking chair with Marvin and sang: *"Bye baby bunting, Daddy's gone a-hunting to get a little rabbit's skin to wrap his baby bunting in."*
"Daddy sing, 'pat-a-cake'," requested Ernie.
"Pat-a-cake, pat-a-cake, baker's man-Make me a cake as fast as you can; Pat it and prick it, and mark it with B-Put it in the oven for Baby and me."
"Pee-pee won't com' out," reported Ernie.
"Well hop back in your bed then."
"Good, I am sleepy," yawned Ernie.
"One last song, Marv's almost out. *"Hush-a-bye, my baby, slumber time is comin' soon; Rest your head upon my knee while Father hums a tune; The sandman is callin' where shadows are fallin'; while soft breezes sigh as in days long gone by."*
Palmer was sure Alice was sleeping by now, so he tiptoed over to the mirror and tried to brush his unruly, wavy hair.
"It won't do any good," yawned Alice.
"How did you know I was brushing my hair?"
"Because you always stand in front of that mirror and try to straighten those waves. The more you brush it, the wavier it gets."
"Don't say that, Mrs. Helgren with your lovely straight-as-a-pin hair."
Alice whispered, "Get in the bed before you wake up the boys."
Palmer lay down. "This bed never felt so good!"
Ernie called, "Daddy, I gotta go pee now!"

"So much for blessed rest," giggled Alice.

Chapter 34   Bittersweet

Spring of 1930

After the long cold winter, signs of spring were a welcome sight. Palmer was up at the first light of dawn. He had made it a habit to "make hay while the sun shines." Palmer had been having abdominal pain and bouts of soreness off and on for the last two weeks. The pain felt more intense today, but he could tolerate it. It was time to plant corn and he must keep moving forward. Here it was the 28th of April and he still had many acres to plant. The growing season here in northern Iowa was short and there was no time to lose. Palmer headed to the barn to milk Daisy. Alice usually milked during planting season, but she was heavy with child and the baby was due any day now.

As Palmer let Daisy out to pasture, light was starting to fill the sky and it streaked the dewy grass with a dazzling gold. Daisy charged into the pasture eager to get a mouthful of that sweet, succulent, spring grass.

Palmer breathed in the cool spring air. It felt so good on his fever ravaged body. As Palmer stooped to pick up the milk pail, the pain in his side became excruciating! Deep penetrating pain coursed through his entire body, but he struggled to force it out of his mind. He started toward the house. His body felt like a raging inferno! If only he could get to the pump and get a cool drink. He set down the milk pail and tried to hold his trembling hands steady. His body felt like a broken city wall seized by invaders. His head pounded with an agonizing headache. Palmer felt his strength waning and he was becoming weaker with every labored breath. He flinched at the stabbing pain in his side! Palmer tried to concentrate on putting one foot in front of the other. His muscles felt like they were burning and twitching. Intense fear gripped Palmer as he dropped to his knees. He tried to crawl, but his body was paralyzed with pain and tremors. He tried to call out with his horror-stricken voice, but no words came. His head was spinning and he was falling, ever falling into a black bottomless pit. He tried to move, but there was only pain and darkness. Exhausted, he collapsed in the yard. Palmer fought to remain conscious, but his mind flooded with blackness.

"Mommy, how come Max is barking?" asked Marvin.

Alice was at the stove frying bacon. "I suppose the pigs are out again," sighed Alice.

"I'll see," said Ernie running to the door. "Mommy come quick," he screamed! "Daddy fell down!"

Ernie and Marvin burst through the door and ran to their father's side! Alice shoved the skillet to the back of the stove and followed the boys as quickly as her tried legs could carry her. Faithful Max, lie next to his master's pale and lifeless body. Alice knelt down beside Palmer. Her full womb pressed against his firm muscular chest as she put her cheek close to his parched lips. She felt his warm breath, he was still alive.

"Ernie get me some water from the pump. Daddy's burning up with fever!" Alice ripped a strip of fabric from her faded apron as Ernie returned with the bucket of water. Strands of Palmer's wavy blonde hair clung to his fiery, red face. Alice laid the wet, cool cloth over his forehead. Palmer moaned and opened his fever glazed eyes as Alice took a deep shuddering breath.

"Palmer save your strength, don't try to talk."

Palmer struggled to fight off the unconsciousness. Alice was saying something, but he felt himself fading away. He could not understand what she said, because he was drifting away like a boat moving out to sea.

"Boys stay with Daddy! Talk to him, hold his hand. I've got to call for help!" Alice ran to the house with her arms holding up the weight of her unborn child. Tremors of fear shook her body as she fought of tears that threatened her self-control. *You must be strong for Palmer and the boys! Be courageous and strong!*

~~~~~~

Alice paced back and forth, back and forth in the hospital waiting room. Martha offered words of comfort that were gentle and supportive. The aching in Alice worried heart refused to abate. Alice closed her eyes and tried to imagine this was not happening.

Finally, Dr. Matthews appeared and John asked, "How is Palmer doing?" although he dreaded to hear the answer.

Dr. Matthews shook his head. "We removed his appendix, but it's too late," he replied honestly. "Palmer is very weak. The gangrene has taken its toll. He's a strong man, but I'm not sure he will make it through the night. His body is too spent to continue the fight." They could sense the undercurrent of anger and frustration in the doctor's voice. "There's nothing that can be done. I'm so very sorry! I'll do what I can to make him comfortable."

The shock of it all ripped at Alice's heart until she could hardly breathe. Her insides quaked and fear and desperation overtook her. Alice wanted to deny the truth. *No hope for my beloved husband. It can't be true, it just cannot be true!*

Alice hit the lowest ebb of her life! The thought of losing Palmer shook her to the very foundation of her being. Tears clouded her vision and she was too stunned to say a word. The light of hope which she had kept burning, failed to return now. She wore a defeated look on her face. Alice struggled to overcome her tumulus waves of emotions, which were surging and churning, swirling and crashing. Alice collapsed into her mother's arms and she shook with every shuddering breath. Tobia held Alice close and they swayed back and forth as she tried to console her daughter with a voice full of gentle sympathy.
Alice's voice quaked as she cried, "Mother, I feel like my heart has been run through with a sword!" Alice tried to hold back the tears, but it was like reversing the course of a raging river!
Ed felt powerless and looked on in helpless frustration as a big tear rolled down his cheek.
Alice knew what she needed to do. Time was not on her side. She would go home and take some castor oil and then start chopping wood. Palmer must see his daughter. He had already named her Helen Margaret after his baby sister.

~~~~~~

Helen was born April 29, 1930, at 2:45.
"I need to get back to the hospital," begged Alice.
"Doter, ye need to rest!" insisted Tobia.
Alice's face drooped with weariness as she cried, "I'll not rest until Palmer sees his daughter!" Short sobs escaped from deep within Alice's heart as her eyes brimmed with tears of exhaustion.
Ed replied sympathetically, "Ye rest fer von hour. Den I tak' ye back to Mason City. I git Eli to do chores ag'in."

~~~~~~

It seemed like eons since Alice had seen Palmer. Her mind was jumbled and she worked to untangle her grief. Her thoughts sank into a deep, dark chasm leaving irreparable scars on her crushed heart. Alice fell wearily into Palmer's arms and kissed his parched lips.
"I've got hot lips now, for my daisy in the wheat field," smiled Palmer.
Alice returned, "You're one firecracker, always have been."
Marvin spouted, "Daddy you're hot!"

"The nurses think so," grinned Palmer. "They love my wavy blonde hair."
Alice added, "And don't forget your beautiful sky-blue eyes."
"We wanted to bring Max," explained Ernie, "but Mommy said he can't come in the hospital."
"Ernie you take care of Max for me."
"I will Daddy," promised Ernie.
"Marvin, can you help Mommy take care of your new sister?"
"Of course, I can," replied Marvin.
"I can help, too," offered Ernie. "I'll sing her a lullaby."
Tobia put baby Helen in Palmer's arms. Helen wrapped her tiny fingers around her father's finger. Palmer smiled at Alice and asked, "Did you name her Helen Margaret?"
"Palmer you were right, it was a little girl. I think she should be named after her father. What if we add an e onto your name and call her Helen Palmere?"
"I would be honored. Helen Palmere has my blue eyes."
"Ja, and your wavy hair," smiled Alice.
"Oh no, it's a good thing she's a girl."
Alice nodded, "She'll look so beautiful with her wavy hair, just like her father's."
Alice was filled with bittersweet joy. Palmer had the adorable daughter that he had always wanted. But Palmer would never see her grow up into a lovely young lady. And Helen would never have the joy of being raised by such a loving father. Alice looked fearfully into Palmer's tired eyes. And Palmer looked back with worried concern. Alice wore a weariness that attested to her extreme exhaustion. Palmer cupped Alice's quivering face in his once strong hands and said tenderly, "You have to go home and rest! Boys, take your mother and baby Helen home and put them to bed."
"We'll do it Daddy," nodded Marvin.
Ernie added, "We'll even sing them a lullaby!"
As the dark days passed, Alice Heart clung to her young sons who looked up into her face with their father's blue eyes. Alice gathered Ernie and Marvin into her arms like chicks under her protective wings. Palmer's strength had always fortified her and now she wanted to pass that on to her sons. Nights were long as Alice pined for Palmer. It was an impossible void to fill. Grief returned at startling dark moments when past memories flooded her mind. Alice was suffocating from a crushed heart and she felt so utterly alone. There was nothing left, but total emptiness. If only she could lose her sadness for just a moment.

Every day they made the trip to the hospital to see Palmer. And every day Alice saw her beloved husband's strength rapidly failing. *Be strong, be courageous and strong!* Alice fought to keep her smile in place. She did not want Palmer to know how hard this was for her. Alice placed baby Helen in her father's arms.

"Palmer you have so many friends. At least half of King township is at our house today putting in our crops. You are beloved by so many!"

"The nurses claim I have way too many visitors, so please thank them for me." Alice nodded gravely, words seemed too drain her of what little strength she had left.

"Alice, my parents bought that little farm at the top of the hill in Thompson. They would like to help you raise our children. That house at the bottom of the hill on the corner is for sale. Father said it has indoor plumbing, electricity, three bedrooms, a good basement and a garage. Oh, and it has a chicken coop too, if you want to keep the chickens." Palmer's soothing voice offered Alice the comfort and strength she needed.

"That house is just a few blocks from the school and the children can walk. And Palmer, I love that front porch."

"I can see you living there with the whole yard full of flowers," smiled Palmer.

"I'll be sure to plant lots of daisies just for you."

"Be sure you leave enough room for your garden," grinned Palmer.

"Oh, I can plant the daisies all around the garden. They'll make a beautiful border."

"Well if you run out of space you can buy the hayfield just south of the house," smiled Palmer. "Father is going to keep a milk cow, so you can send one of the children up the hill with the syrup can to get fresh milk daily. Alice, do you remember Peter and Eliza Olson?"

"Ja, aren't they the folks that want to buy our farm?"

"Yes and their offer still stands. And it's a good offer Alice. So go look at that house, pray about it and I'm sure you'll know what to do by morning."

~~~~~~

Alice returned home with a sinking heart. She loved the house in Thompson, especially the indoor plumbing. But the thought of living there without Palmer blurred her eyes with sudden tears. She was living in a shroud of dark despair with a heart wrenched with pain and grief. She felt too weary to go on. Alice realized she could no longer cope with this trial. It was a burden too heavy to bear in her own strength. She needed divine help. With blinding tears that blurred her vision she stumbled through the woods to Palmer's thinking log. Alice wept until she could weep no more. She remembered the scripture at 1 John 3:20, "God is greater than our hearts and knows all things." From her deep despair, she cried out to her Heavenly Father. She poured out her heart asking for comfort, wisdom and strength to cope with this trial. To heal the deep wounds in her crushed heart, so she could endure the pain. She begged for help to remove the fears and uncertainty and to make the way ahead clear. Alice felt a peace come over her that she had not even dared to hope for. With her strength renewed, Alice was sure that she could now move forward. Alice realized that she would always long for the love she had lost, for what could have been. There would always be an empty space in her heart, a space that Palmer would leave behind. But Palmer would want her to move on, and to build around that space. When she looked back at her life with Palmer, it had been nothing, but boundless joy! Alice had the undeniable feeling that she had been blessed beyond what she could have ever imagined! The lost light of hope was gradually returning to Alice's face. Alice stopped at the big cottonwood tree and said her good-byes. Alice knew now that she needed to buy the house in Thompson. John and Martha had done a fine job raising Palmer and his wonderful siblings. She would humbly accept their help. It was the answer to her prayer.

~~~~~~

It was May 5, 1930, and Palmer's life sifted slowly away like the streaming sand in an hour-glass. Palmer was so tired, so very weary of fighting. His raging fever consumed him and he only wanted to be free of his misery. Palmer took Alice into his arms. She looked into the blue eyes that had always bathed her in love. Palmer's eyes were a storm of hurt and caring. His touch was gentle as he stroked Alice hair. "Alice, it's not the dying that's hard, it's the living. Be courageous and strong for me and our children. I know I can count on you. Alice you are an amazing women and there is nothing you cannot do!"
The love and warmth in Palmer's voice bolstered Alice's courage and she spoke in a calm voice that masked the dread in her heart. "Palmer, I'm grateful that in this life, I was loved by you." Alice tenderly kissed him and Palmer felt her tears wet his cheeks as she clung to her beloved. Alice gently wiped her tears from his face. "I love you Palmer Olai Helgren!"
Palmer whispered, "I will always love you, my daisy in the wheat field." THE END

Palmer died beloved by all. His gentle ways and bright smile touched the lives of many. His kindness and generosity were not easily forgotten!

In the autumn of 1929, the stock market crashed. A decade of Great Depression lay ahead for America. Half of the banks in the USA failed. A quarter of a million Americans found themselves unemployed as towns and industries dried up. Severe drought turned the land into a dust bowl and locusts finished off any crops that had survived. It was a time to be conservative and nothing was thrown away. A time to be inventive and creative with whatever you had. Mothers learned to "make a silk purse from a sow's ear." In the kitchen, they turned almost nothing into something to eat. They became skilled at turning rejected clothing into something that looked brand new. Food was as scarce as money. People learned to survive for days on bread and milk gravy. Corn meal was a staple and mothers turned it into an all-time favorite, Buttermilk Johnny Cake.

Alice was one of those Depression mothers who did whatever it took to help her children survive. She grew all of her own garden produce. She sewed feed-sacks into clothes. Alice taught by example that caring and sharing was a way of life. Alice raised three remarkable children during the Great Depression. Palmer was right all along. Alice was an amazing woman and there was nothing she could not do!

Made in the USA
Monee, IL
25 January 2021